Roland Johnson's
LOST IN A DESERT WORLD

AN AUTOBIOGRAPHY
(as told to Karl Williams)

© 1994 Roland Johnson and Karl Williams

Published by Speaking For Ourselves
Philadelphia, PA

Cover and Book Design by WildNess Graphic Design

Some names of individuals have been changed.

ISBN 978-0-578-73082-0

"Roland Johnson was one of the first self-advocates I ever met — that is, one of the first individuals to emerge from the formal disability system, to proclaim to the world that he was ready, willing and certainly able to articulate his own priorities, and to represent the interests of his friends. When he spoke, his courage, eloquence and ability to turn adversity into positive action moved all present. His death cut short an extraordinary life — but one that left us all with more humility and understanding in the face of his example."

Val Bradley, President, Human Services Research Institute
and Chair, President's Committee on MR.

"Roland Johnson was my friend. He was the most fascinating person I have ever known. The first time I met Roland he said ... 'Steve Eidelman, I want to tell you that we have people in institutions who we are worried about. Can you help them get out?' The last time I spoke with Roland was a few months before he died. He said the same thing. And every time in-between. I thought I knew Roland. After reading his story, I realize I knew only a part of him. A small part. Roland always to took me to task. It was his job to do so, and my job to take it. When he talked, somehow, it carried more weight then the paid advocates I dealt with. He was so fervent in his beliefs and so skilled in talking about the people he cared so much about. Roland's story mirrors the amazing changes in our country in the past fifty years for people with mental retardation. Much of what he tells we would rather forget. But we cannot. And we cannot fool ourselves into thinking it can't happen again. It can and does. Imagine what Roland could have accomplished if he were born today. A man with such gifts could have done even more remarkable things then the remarkable things told in Roland' story. I miss him."

Steve Eidelman, past Deputy Secretary for MR, Pennsylvania, Executive Director, ARC, USA

"It's exciting to have a book about Roland Johnson in Roland's words. He was an effective advocate speaking before committees of the legislature, at press conferences, conventions, anywhere we needed him. Roland believed that no one should have to live in an institution — he knew because he had lived there — and he worked diligently for quality community living arrangements. He spoke forcefully, sensitively and with dignity. Roland said that we can all learn from each other. With his book he can continue to teach us."

Eleanor Elkin, Past President, ARC, USA

CONTENTS

People who produce autobiographies often have no need that their significance be explained. But unless you are familiar with something called the self-advocacy movement, chances are you have not heard the name Roland Johnson before.

The fact that was central to Roland Johnson's history — and so to the contribution he made during his lifetime — was that he had a disability, what was called during his life — and is still often referred to as — mental retardation.

In the white male Eurocentric world of the last few centuries women and people whose skin happened not to be white were considered somewhat less than fully human — those in control did not expect anything of value to come from either direction.

If in this century those prejudices have begun to disappear, there is still prejudice enough left to fill in.

You are now holding in your hands a book in which a man who had mental retardation tells about his life. Between these pages is all the evidence anyone should need to convince them that there is most definitely something of value to be found in people with this disability. It may be difficult to put into words exactly what that something is. It has nothing to do with what we now define as intelligence — or with wealth or power or physical attractiveness. People with this disability by definition have a lower than average IQ; they are also usually poor, powerless, and by the world's standards somewhat less than attractive physically. But because it may be a bit elusive, this contribution they have to make — this world we find ourselves living in today being so completely driven by intellect, money, power, and beauty — because this contribution may be difficult to put one's finger on, that does not mean that it does not exist.

When I met Roland Johnson he was the president of Speaking For Ourselves, a group of self-advocates, i.e., people with disabilities engaged in the newest outcropping of the civil rights movement.

I write songs; I heard a keynote speaker at Speaking For Ourselves' annual conference ask how there could be a movement without music; and I suggested that I try writing a song for them.

They asked me to come and meet with them to talk about my proposal.

It was a most unusual scene.

The headquarters of Speaking For Ourselves is in a high-rise office building just outside Philadelphia. On my way in I'd passed two men in three-piece suits with briefcases. And now I sat at one end of a long table flanked by some of the members of the Board of Directors of Speaking For Ourselves who would consider my suggestion. A man came into the room using the kind of crutches with cuffs that the forearms slip into. The room was just large enough for the long table and chairs and when I saw where he was headed, I got up to move my chair out of the way for him.

"You're the song writer," he said with an engaging smile that almost closed his eyes.

I noticed as he passed me that he'd missed a small area under his ear on his right jaw when he'd shaved that morning.

The shirt he wore worked its way out of his pants at the side from his exertion in getting to and sitting down in the chair on the side of the table to my left, and when he came to rest finally, his tie was askew as well. He seemed to me to be unaware of this — or maybe he just didn't care.

He made a comment to the woman across the table as he put his crutches on the floor and laughed — a bit louder than the room seemed designed for — at his own words.

I didn't get the joke.

And I thought that she didn't either.

As we went back to waiting for the meeting to begin, what little small talk that passed among the others around the table seemed to me somehow to miss connecting just as this joke had. I didn't know what to say to anyone, but then neither did any of the members.

One man had a set of earphones on his head and kept busy adjusting the station on the portable radio to which they were attached — so that he appeared to be all but oblivious to anything that was said.

A short and very heavy woman made her way towards a chair to my right with a Styrofoam cup of some beverage in her hand. She tilted from foot to foot in order to propel herself forward — and I was mildly amazed when she did in fact come to rest in her seat with the contents of her cup still completely within the confines of the cup.

A man who looked as if he hadn't combed his hair that day made it a point to let me know — it took me a moment to understand that he was in fact addressing me — that he was doing this (he meant his involvement with Speaking For Ourselves) "for my nieces and nephews — for the younger ones who'll come after."

There was something the world would call "different" — and the word would be used in a negative sense — about each of the people around this table. The immediately apparent difference was made up of a mixture of physical appearance, grooming, choice of clothing. The underlying difference subsequently revealed itself in choice of words, in language, in assumptions about life. But in essence, I've come to see, the real mixture has more to do with who these folks are and with what the world has tried to do to them because of who they are.

So here we all sat around this table in this meeting room in this office to which the five county chapters of Speaking For Ourselves had sent representatives to the Board of Directors.

At the other end of the table Roland Johnson took his place and started the meeting.

And an hour and a half later I came out of that room with their OK to take a shot at writing that song — and with the distinct impression that I'd just witnessed something that was supposed to be impossible: I'd attended a meeting of people the world had long ago decided did not have the wherewithal to conduct such a meeting.

And Roland Johnson had chaired that meeting.

And not only had the meeting come off, but things had gone in a most unique — though I saw expedient — fashion. People had come and gone in the middle of things to use the bathroom or get a drink; what was obviously a running joke among the members of the group about the ability — or lack thereof — of one of the advisors to keep his life together was visited for, I could tell, the umpteenth time and everyone laughed; I was asked to step outside for a time, after I'd spoken, while they discussed what I'd said. As it was happening, it seemed to me that nothing was happening. But in reality I left with their instructions to attend several of their chapter meetings, so that I had a good idea what

the group was all about, before I started working on the song.
Despite how it had seemed to me — despite what my own deep-
seated prejudice wanted to convince me of — afterwards I could
see that it all made perfect sense.

• • •

In order that you be adequately prepared to encounter Roland
Johnson here in print, it will be necessary for you first to rid
yourself of your preconceptions.

Yes, he was a member of that group of people you remember
catching a glimpse of down that corridor at your high school
which you or your friends might have gone out of your way to
avoid, the one at the end of which was located the special ed
classroom.

Most likely you have read a book or seen a movie in which
someone with this disability is portrayed. But a character like
Lenny in "Of Mice & Men" or Benjy in "The Sound and the
Fury" or Forrest Gump is a figure not meant to represent reality;
such a figure is quasi-allegorical, created by a writer hoping to
say something, not so much about his or her creation, as about
the human condition.

The man you will meet in these pages was a real human being
who lived in the same real world we all inhabit.

In order to meet Roland Johnson, you must allow for the
possibility of the impossible.

In order to find a treasure, you must at the very least not deny,
however slim, the chance of its existence.

In order to see the humanity in Roland Johnson you must first
reconnect with your own.

• • •

We haven't wanted to know about people like Roland Johnson and so, fifty or forty or even thirty years ago — and in some places this same advice is still likely to be heard even today — when a baby was born with developmental disabilities, the doctor would invariably counsel the parents to put their son or daughter away and forget about them.

Roland Johnson's mother and father did not take this advice. But they had no one to help them — no counselors, no psychologists, no therapists, no teachers. And when the problems that Roland's disability presented began to overwhelm them, what with the eight other children they had to provide and care for, they had only one choice — to resign themselves to that initial recommendation.

"Away" meant an institution, what was often called a state "school." But if the founders of such facilities had envisioned some kind of rehabilitative education, it was most often a very different kind of instruction those incarcerated there received.

Roland Johnson was sexually assaulted soon after he moved into Pennhurst State School outside Philadelphia. Through his teen age years he was hospitalized repeatedly for venereal disease, the result of the clandestine sexual activity that was pervasive at the place. He and his fellow inmates were made to do all the real work at Pennhurst: scrubbing floors, caring for the more severely disabled residents, serving food, doing laundry — and none of them was ever paid. He despaired of ever getting out of Pennhurst and it is from his description of his feelings that the title of this book comes.

But he did get out.

And by the time he did the world had begun to change, however slightly and slowly. The long move back to the community that is still going on today was just beginning. But there was no place to move to in the community. And so through the seventies and early eighties he shifted from one makeshift boarding home to another, trying to put his life back together and working through the anger that his years at Pennhurst had left in him. And at the same time he floated in and out of jobs.

During one prolonged jobless period he found himself enrolled in a kind of counseling program at a hospital. Here, under the supervision of doctors, the patients ran their own group. And Roland Johnson discovered in himself an ability to voice the trouble his life and his disability had brought him, while at the same time he also took in the structure and the dynamic of the program.

And so when sometime later he came upon Speaking For Ourselves and was soon elected to the presidency, first of the Philadelphia chapter and then of the Board of Directors, he realized that he had the tools he needed to bring order to what was still in large part chaos.

Self-advocacy was so named to highlight what is most remarkable about this latest development of the civil rights movement which began among black people in the 40s and 50s and spread in succeeding decades to other devalued groups: women, gays, the variously physically disabled. Self-advocacy is the name for the phenomenon of people, defined as lacking the ability to think for themselves, not only thinking but speaking out — to each other in comfort and solidarity and to the world in demand of their rights under the law.

Speaking For Ourselves started in Philadelphia and quickly spread. At the same time similar groups were springing up in other states and in other countries.

In the years that followed his ascendancy in Speaking For Ourselves Roland Johnson went on to speak to struggling self-advocacy groups in other states and countries and to organizations of the professionals who provide services to people with disabilities.

He spoke of the evils inherent in the system he grew up in. But he spoke with a magnanimity that belied the suffering he'd endured. He spoke of his vision for the future, of a world where people like himself could be treated as full human beings.

Roland Johnson was a man of great courage and vision and determination. He had what can be called an alternate kind of intelligence — one that is not based on the ability to manipulate data, what we call intellect. In Roland Johnson's world understanding — one person for another — is the way of the future, the only route to true freedom.

Though virtually unknown in his lifetime outside the world of self-advocacy, he was a pioneer: his life traced a path no one had trod before — he escaped the hell his disability had consigned him to and went on to organize and speak out on behalf of his brothers and sisters.

• • •

What I contributed to this project was my ability to manipulate data. Roland Johnson and I tape recorded hours of conversation about his life. Speaking For Ourselves paid for the transcription of those tapes. I took out all my questions and comments and worked entirely and exclusively with Roland Johnson's words. What you will read is an authentic voice: I put no words in Roland Johnson's mouth. What I did was only to bring some order to that which is erratic in each of us, the memory of our own existence.

My hope is that you will hear Roland Johnson's voice as you read these pages; that you will take heed of what he tells you; and that, as you read his words, that peculiar brand of embarrassment with which the world now responds to people who are different in the way that he was different will begin to dissipate in you.

We condemn the efforts of some to reshape the world in their own image through such actions as extermination, or what is now referred to as "cleansing." But it still remains for us to step boldly to the opposite path. We have not fully embraced the universe until we have opened our eyes and our hearts to all that it contains. If it is folly to think ourselves gods, then wisdom must lie in accepting all the wonders this world offers. Roland Johnson and his brothers and sisters constitute one of those wonders; may this book open your eyes to that fact.

INTRODUCTION

Roland with his niece in
front of his home in Philadelphia

This book is The Roland Johnson Story — about his life history, his data.

People should be reading this story about people living in institutions and how they been treated. I want to try to help. What can I help to do to give back into the community? This is what I'm struggling very hard to give back: this book would show others how a person been treated and now he has a life to himself.

— Roland Johnson

CHILDHOOD

I smelled biscuits. She would make up her dough and put yeast in the dough and let it sit over night and all that dough would rise and in the morning she would come down and you could smell the biscuits cooking. And all the neighbors would walk by and smell this good food cooking. They'd say, "Grace, what's that smell; it smells very good; could we have some?" She would make that homemade bread and she would just be in there cooking — cooking and cooking while the girls would still be sleeping and I would be awake.

She got up I'd say around about six o'clock, 'cause my father had to go out and work. And during the school days we had to get up early, 'cause we had to be ready at a certain time for school. And special in the mornings she had grits, and scrambled eggs, and pancakes, and bacon, and scrapple, and stuff like that. Biscuits was my favorite smell. We used to just put some syrup over the cornbread.

The house was big — three bedrooms, kitchen, dining room. My mother, my father, all six girls and three boys. Then we moved up on Cleveland Street from South Philly. We had rats crawling around down South Philly on Elsworth Street and we got another house in North Philly, 2435 North Cleveland Street. I remember that. We moved from Elsworth Street to North Philadelphia. My father was looking for another house anyway, because with all them children you gotta have another house.

3

When we was living down on Elsworth street, the girls would be playing when my mother would go out to work, and they'd roll up the toilet paper and get a spoon and wet the toilet paper and throw it at the next-door windows, throw the toilet paper cross people's alley at people's windows. That's how close the houses was. And my mother said, "Where's all this toilet paper gone?" She didn't do nothing with the girls; she just said, "You girls go down to the store and get me some more toilet paper!" They would just be up there just wasting up toilet paper. I wouldn't have no parts of that. All I was doing was busy eating up the food.

They had a mix, mixed people, white and color, in the neighborhood. Back in them days, the neighborhood was quiet. Never was no noise in the neighborhood. And they used to keep the streets nice and clean, the alleys nice and clean. The people used to get out there, sweep off the pavement, wash down their alleys. The neighborhood was so clean back in them days — just sparkling clean. But now, today they don't do it.

My mother went to church with me and my sisters; on Elsworth Street, Christian Union; it was just right across the street from us; the pastor's name was Brother Ervine. She dressed me up to go to church when I was a little boy in a little suit and a little hat and little shoes and a bow tie. I liked that very much. I always wanted to go to church, It was very exciting to go to church. All of my sisters went to Sunday School. I went to Sunday School every Sunday.

It was kind of older, a small church, and a large congregation, and every time they would see me, "Oh, there's that Roland Johnson. He will eat! He will eat!" I had a good reputation. Everybody knew me — we used to go to the Sunday School

4

picnic. To go to church, that was my favorite thing. A lot of people knew me from going to church; they knew me when I was small.

My father never went to church. My mother wore a dress and beads; she wore earrings; she wasn't too much in lipstick. She'd wear a hat, different hats every Sunday. She taught Sunday School class at Christian Union. My mother would not allow cards and our father wouldn't have cards in the house. My mother was always a very church-going person.

I always sat out on the steps in the summertime. My mother used to dress me in shorts and a shirt and socks and told me to sit out on the steps. My mother said, "Stay right there in the middle of the front step." I didn't suck my thumb; I used to suck these two fingers.

I remember we used to sit out on the steps up until nine o'clock; nine thirty we had to go to bed. We had to be in the house by nine thirty. My mother would give me a bath, put me to bed, and then put the girls to bed.

We had a porch on Elsworth Street. On Cleveland Street it was just a house with no porch, just steps, four, five, six steps, made out of concrete, and a black railing. The kids would play hide-and-go-seek, hit-the-man, or catch-the-man. The girls jumped rope; I seen them jump rope, sitting on the summer steps.

You wouldn't sit on those steps on Sundays, either. Sunday was a special day. Only during the week, you could sit on those steps. People would come and visit, but you could never sit on the steps on Sundays. Sundays was the Christian, then.

We used to play Indians and hide-and-go-seek with the next-door neighbor, until his mother called him in the house. This was during the summer. In the winter snow would be this high — we still had to go to school; they didn't call no school off.

I had a great-grandfather and a great-grandmother. They was living on Elsworth Street with us til they got sick. That was my mother's grandfather and grandmother. They was very ill. They went to the hospital and I don't know what hospital they went to. They died. I don't remember a funeral, 'cause I was doing my thing, getting into trouble. I don't remember them.

My father and mother met up in Philadelphia together and they got married; he was from Richmond, Virginia. My father fixed things. There was no arguments with the family — who fixes this and who fixes that. Sometimes my mother would fix it, put things together. They got along together. No disagreements. There was no marriage broke up or nothing. No divorce.

All the girls did the cleaning. My mother 'signed them: Bertha May would do the bathroom; Beatrice would help to do the dishes one night; the other girls would do the dishes the next night and clean up the kitchen; Bernie would take out the trash; one night I would take out the trash. Sometimes I wash the dishes or cleaned the kitchen too. My mother would feed the cats and dog.

Laverne always wanted the pets. She cried because she wanted a pet. And my father said, "Girl, shut up. Would you shut up, please? Stop talking about the pets; we have enough of our own." And she cried and she pestered and she cried and she pestered and she said, "Mom, I think we need a pet around." So my mother took her to the SPCA, and so we had a cat and a dog and a little chicken. They built a chicken house and a fence out in the yard. And the cat and the dog did not let other cats in the yard. Toby would chase the cats out of there.

My father worked on cars and my mother went out to work housekeeping. Back in them days, we had a struggle. I was born 1945, right after the war. They had to really work hard to make ends meet. It wasn't quite as hard as they have today, but, with the girls and with the boys that she had, she had to struggle. We had to make sure that the dishes was washed and the food was cooked before she came home. My older sister was in charge of that, Vera. She kind of ran the house. I remember all my sisters took care of me when I was small. And that, when I got into trouble, that's when I got beaten.

My Mama told the girls, "When I go out to work, you better have them dishes done. When I come back, you better have the food cooked and done, and watch that boy." Me. Roland. "Watch that Roland. Don't let him out of your sight."

I can never forget my sister says, "You better watch this boy, 'cause Mom put you in charge, to watch him." And they said, "Well, you're the one who's supposed to watch him!" "Well, Mom didn't put me in charge to watch him. He's sneaking off in that kitchen!" They would be watching TV and I would be sneaking, just sneaking, just one step, sneaking, and crawling and into the kitchen. They say, "Better watch Roland, because I'm not watching him! He's too fast for me." I would be quick — in the kitchen. That fast.

Vera was the first child born. Her name was Vera, but we call her Sissy. Then my brother, William, was born after Sissy. And then Boopsie was born right behind William. And then Bertha May. I was sleeping on the bottom of the bed and then the girls would sleep up on top, the head of the bed. We all fit in the bed together and Laverne slept with my father and mother when she was small. The other girls slept in the back room, and the brothers.

I'm the last child that my mother had, although I had a twin. Madeleine had a twin and I had a twin, but the twins died in crib death.

Laverne was my favorite sister. She would take me out places. We would get dressed up on Halloween and go out trick-or-treating. I think I was dressed up as a hobo. We went to church together and we went to school together. And we went to movies together. Yeah and we would walk to the railroad tracks; it was not real close to our house — we had to walk down over a bridge and walk near a park.

If someone would ax me, "What you want to do, as you grow up?" I would say first I wanted to be a fireman, put out the fires and stuff. If I had someone ax me today, if I was small, "What would you want to do when you grow up," I would say I wanted to be a minister or a doctor, help people that was very sick. Or if I went to school, if I could read, and went to college and learn something from books, maybe I could see through it more, what my life is about, make people understand who I am, and where I come from, what I stood for. The family didn't push nothing, they didn't push the issue. They just thought that I was a person that could do anything: "Roland could do anything; if he want to; if he would put his mind down to it."

William got almost run over by a horse and buggy. They was selling ice; we had an icebox. Back in them days, we didn't have icetrays — we used to get ice from the iceman.

William snuck in the service; he was too young. I remember a man from the military service — he had some badge on himself — he came at the door; he axed my mother, "Did you know your son was in the service?" And my father said, "Well, what son are you talking about?" "Your son signed up for the service." He drafted himself into the service. That was William — he come home and he said, "Mom, I'm in the service, look at me!" My father got on him. "Boy, why didn't you tell me? The cops was out here." They had badges and stripes and my mother was scared — and my father was scared too. He stayed in the service. He got shot in the leg; he had one toe shot off; I didn't see that — my mother told me. Then he worked for Frank's Canada Dry. He drive a truck. And he was a minister and he met his wife.

Now Bernie, he was a type of spoiled little child; he got everything his way all the time; my mother used to pet him up a little. Every time he does something, she would back him out of things. When he got bitten by a dog, he was running home and saying, "Mom, Mom, I got bit!" and my mother had to take him to the doctor. He said, "I don't want to go!" And she said, "Boy, you better shut up. There ain't nothing bothering you. You've just got a big cut and I'll take you to the doctor." And all my sisters was just saying, "All she do is just spoil that boy. That boy get everything; Bernie get everything his way." If he wanted something, he got it. If he wanted the car — this is when he was big — he got the car. He didn't have any driving license yet, so he got the car and he stayed out late and that's when my father got really mad; he got a real beating from my father. Nobody else got a beating. The next-door neighbor hear him getting a beating; this was on Cleveland Street. My father told him he had to be in the house at a certain time, and he disobeyed. My father stayed up that night, waiting for him, turned all the lights out in the living room and the kitchen. When Bernie snuck in the window, that's when my father really gave it to him. He had the whole neighborhood woke up. My Mama came down the stairs and she said, "Roy, stop doing that. Don't beat him! That's enough, that's enough!" He never did it again, Bernie. My father was that built and strong.

It was very good, through my good childhood. It was very good for my brothers and sisters. We had fun, and like I said, we used to play ring-around-the-rosy … My mother and father was really strict. And we better not have said a boo. When we had guests at the house, we better not be sitting in the parlor; you could never sit down and listen to conversations they had. No, they were strict.

I never forget the time when Laverne brought Walt Cheatham around the house. My father looked up and down at him and wanted to know if this was the right person to be engaged with. My father gave Walt the eye, up and down, sized him up and down. Walt walked in the kitchen and opened the icebox and my father says, "You don't come in my house and open up the icebox; who do you think you are? You don't come in my house and open up the 'frigerator and look in my 'frigerator. This is not your house." And Laverne had to die laughing at him. My mother didn't say nothing. And then they got along together after that and they got married.

Bernie used to pull me in the wagon. He would collect papers, newspapers, and sell it, try to make some money off of it. He was picking up old papers. He brought me back home and then he sold the papers to a junk man.

Bernie played football out to the playground, 'cross from Connie Mack Stadium. There was a playground there. His friends used to just knock on the door and ax my mother, "Is Bernie home, can he come out?" "Yeah, he can, but he has to eat first."

Sometime he took me to a playground and Connie Mack Stadium, to the ball game. My father took us all to Atlantic City — that's before the casinos; they had games down Atlantic City — my aunts, my mother's sister and his brother, they drove in different cars and went down Atlantic City. We had a good time. And at night we would come back for a box of saltwater taffies. My mother would buy three boxes — one box, a big box, wouldn't last — not around me, anyway.

Around Easter time I would get in and eat up Madeleine's candy, that's my other sister. She had a diet candy. Oh boy she was mad at me. Oh, she was angry. She said, "Mom, that boy ate all my diet candy." Then my Mama said, "I don't know what to do with the boy." Yeah, it wasn't bad; it was the days.

My aunt had three boys and six girls, just like my mother. We all got together for holidays. We had a Thanksgiving dinner, Christmas dinner. My mother got up in the morning, she'd go to church and she would be cooking in the afternoon. She would fix a big dinner, at Thanksgiving, and have us all, and I think she had thirteen sisters and brothers on her side of the family, and my father had two brothers. I felt pretty happy when all the people come over, because they used to give me quarters and dimes and nickels.

My father thought I had nice wavy hair. He had nice wavy hair. My mother would plait up his hair and it would come out just wavy; it'd be nice. All the boys' hairs used to be like that in the family, and the girls'. And a friend of my father's he used to come cut my head. Every two weeks. And he used to give me quarters. He would pick me up and say, "How you doing, Roland?" I liked that. He would give me some money. My mother would say, "Don't give that boy no money, don't give him nothing. He's bad, he don't need none." I never forget that guy; he give all my sisters each a dime or quarter or fifty cents, each of them. I went into the store. At that time I didn't think about piggy banks, saving it up. I would get like taffies. It was penny apiece back in them days.

Back in them days they used to call it the whooping cough, that you couldn't get rid of. She'd give me some onions, cook 'em, and put 'em in the rag; she would get a whole rag and put it around your neck. That would try to get rid of colds. If that didn't work, she would get some tea bags and put it in a rag, heat it up some, and rub it on your neck, all in your chest, and that kind of took down the fever. I mostly had the highest fever in the family. Or she would heat the bottle up, of mineral oil, and she would rub it all over your chest, and give you cough medicine.

I would break out and she didn't know what it was coming from. My lips was all swollen, eyes was all puffed up. She'd take me to the doctor. And the doctor says, "Well, Mrs. Johnson, your son's got the hives from the onions. Don't give him no more onions." So that kind of stopped.

Back in the fifties we was looking at *Mickey Mouse, Donald Duck, I Love Lucy, Rin Tin Tin, Lone Ranger, Hopalong Cassidy, Billy the Kid* and *I Bet Your Life*. They had a floor model TV. One upstairs, in the bedroom, and one downstairs. Black and white. Back in them days they didn't have colored ones. I know them days, 'cause my niece, Pinky, would come over after school and spend an evening over, and all she wanted to watch — *Mickey Mouse*. And if the girls didn't turn on *Mickey Mouse* for her, she would ax my mother, "Grandmom, they won't turn on *Mickey Mouse* for me." So my Mom said, "You better put that *Mickey Mouse* on. Before I come in there." So they turned it on.

Back in them times you couldn't get too many things for Christmas. I wanted a trike, a tricycle. I wanted — what is it — some kind of toy that showed up on TV. I axed for that, but

I didn't get it. My mother just bought me a wagon and a fire truck. And clothes. She got a big fire truck, about this long. Ladders and holes — like a real fire truck. That made me happy when I got the fire truck.

'Round Christmas time I used to bring a great big Christmas tree home; I would swipe it from the store. They had the trees outside and I would bring it home. My mother says to my father, "Would you look at this boy? Would you look at this boy? He's got a tree and didn't pay for it." My father said, "Boy, you take that tree right back down there where you got it from." And Laverne says, "Please can we keep that tree? Please?" And my mother said, "That tree ain't paid for." So Dad, my father, went down and paid for the tree. It was a big, tall tree — this big. He got a stand and put the tree up. That's when I was very, very young.

We decorated the house; put lights up outside the windows, inside the windows; put Christmas tree lights on, Christmas bulbs on, ornaments; put snowflakes in the windows and snow-flakes around the tree. I remember them days. We would all help to decorate the tree. We put it up Christmas Eve.

I remember Joe; Joe was a white man. He owned a store up in North Philly. Down from him, there's the candy store and the guy from where they sell cabbage and greens and stuff. They all knew me. Mr. Slaughter would tell my mother, "You know that boy of yours, I keep my eyes on him. Every time he comes in, every time you send him to the store, he will be quick and fast, picking up things. He's a very fast person. I don't know how he does it. But he walks out the store with a pocket full of stuff."

Roland was the person getting into everything — just be getting into everything. I'd be nervous 'cause she would find out things and she would keep it to herself — she never said much. But I just knew she would find out sooner or later. I was just like a hungry person, who always had to take things, pick up things. Every time she'd send me to the store, I'd be back with something I didn't buy.

When I was little my mother had to pull my legs to give me some exercise. She took me to the doctor and my legs would go, like, in. And the doctor said, "Mrs. Johnson, if he doesn't walk, he would be paralyzed, from his waist down, if you don't not do the treatment that I 'scribed. The only way that you could get him to walk is by giving him a bath every day and salting his legs everyday, and exercising — make him run up and down the steps, back and forth, make him get up and do some exercise, because his legs were getting twisted." And if she didn't do that, I would have been. Because I didn't want to get up and walk. My mother would always say, "Come on, come on, come on." She'd try to push me to make me walk. And I guess she's sorry that she did push me to make me walk — that's my thinking — I guess she'd say, "Well, I'm sorry that I made him walk, because now I see him getting into everything that he can possible get into." That's why.

I started off in a regular school class and the teacher would write back to my mother on the report card that, "Your son cannot keep up with the other kids in the class. He's very slow. He's a slow learner." They put me in a different class because I couldn't keep up with the other kids' level. It made me feel that either I was weird or neither the teachers was weird. Why would they put me in that type of class? Why would they put me in with the slow, on my level? I guess back there in them days they didn't have no special aides in class. Every time the teacher would crack my hands and make me write letters like A, B, C, D,

I would do like little kids do it. They scribble, instead of writing. Or say the sounds — I just couldn't say the sounds. They would ax me what day of the week was; I didn't know. They would crack my hands. With a yardstick. Like them Catholic sisters used to do. But this was regular school, a public school. I could not keep up with the grade level, so they had to sent me to a special school. I remember making things out of wood and going to music class and we had papers too, to learn how to write our names in cursive. I couldn't do that; I couldn't print, 'cause I was still a little boy. All I could do was just scribble. I don't know what the name of that school was, but anyway, I went to school, but I could not keep up with them, with the grades. I ate my lunch before I got to school and ate up all the rest of the kids' lunch — when it was lunch time I grabbed their lunch when the teacher wasn't looking. And when they had recess I would sneak back up in the class and get a pocketful of cookies. 'Member, them days back then they used to give you cookies and milk at the end of recess, they make you lay down on a cot and come back before the rest in the afternoon, and they give you another recess in the afternoon. I would sneak up there and get some cookies. I knew where they kept the cookies. I couldn't get the milk, but I got to the cookies. I ate the whole big box of cookies. The teachers wanted to know where all the cookies got to. And then they looked at me. They sent a note home to my mother said, "He was a naughty boy today."

When we moved from Elsworth Street to North Philadelphia, it just followed the pattern; it just went along with me. I was kept on taking things.

My sister, Laverne, used to take me to school. She used to wait for me because Mom said, "You gotta take that boy to school." I would get lost. And the school would call up and say, "Mrs. Johnson, your son is not here in the class. Where did he go?" And they would be looking for me. My mother would be looking all over for me. I had the principal all upset and the school all looking for me. My mother would find me in the police station. Eating ice cream.

The police would pick me up. And they would call my mom, and I would be eating ice cream every time she come down to police, and they would give me ice cream, when I was small, was a little thing. And she would say, "Why are they feeding him ice cream?" My father would say, "Well, Grace, I don't know what to do. Our hands are full, our hands are tied." She had full time with me. Raising me and raising the girls and the boys — her hands were full. Working too. And plus my father was working. All my sisters would take care of me. But it was just that Mr. Johnson was into everything; they just couldn't keep up with me.

My sister Bertha May was saving up a whole lot of money, a piggy bank of quarters, nickels, dimes, pennies — until she got a whole jar full — and she would hide it. I knew where she hid it at, behind the sofa. When my mother went to work, I stayed back from school and she thought I was on the school bus. I ran back home and I climbed through the kitchen window — it was cracked in the alleyway — I found this jar — it was heavy — and I'm trying to lift it and I threw the jar across the alleyway.

And she'd be looking behind the couch-sofa for her money, and around behind where my father used to sit in the decliner chair and rocks, and she says, "Mom, did somebody move my piggy bank?" Because my mother used to clean the house up around Christmas; she used to get everything shined up — silverwares, polish her knickknacks and stuff — I would be getting into a lot of things. So I'd have threw her money out in the alley.

My sister went to school with the neighbor's daughter, Joan, from the next door, from the cross from the alley. And she said, "Mom, there's a whole lot of money out here. I don't know where this money comes from. There's a whole lot of money, out in the alley. I wish you'd come and see all this money. And there's comic books!" Because she loved her comics, she loved to read comic books. I threw it all over. And her mother called my mother and said, "Mrs. Johnson, we found a lot of money — did you know did anybody threw some money over our 'cross our alley?" My mother said, "Money? I know my daughter was looking for some money. Well how did it get there?" And Joan's mother said, "Well, you know your son must have been throwing money over the alleyway." "Oh, he has, did he? Oh, so that's where the money got to." So she told me, "Go upstairs." Bertha May was crying with tears. Joan brought some of the money back. It was just, poor Mr. Johnson, got into trouble again. And, "That boy! I can't see why that boy ... There's something the matter with that boy!" It was just ... something just going on. I did it. And didn't knew that I did it. It just happened that way.

One time I jumped out the third-floor window; I jumped out and did not get a scratch on an arm; I didn't get a broken leg. And I opened the gate and I ran out and left the gate open. We had a little dog, Toby, and the dog followed me and he got hit by a car. I was crossing the street and the car was coming up and the light turned and he got — you know how dogs they get scared and they panic — and he got hit by a car. That was the prettiest dog that we had. My mother cried about that dog. And they called and the dog catchers picked him up and took him — I guess they took him and burned him. He couldn't walk. A cop found me. That was on Elsworth Street, I think.

I used to bang my head and stuff like that — on the walls. There was times when I felt lonely, when nobody was around. I just felt nobody cared; nobody would share things with me — and I just felt lonely.

Our house had a parlor and a big kitchen, a living room and a dining room. And there was the shed kitchen; the shed kitchen had shelves and cabinets and a door and windows. It had another door that you go out in the yard and it had a door when you go in, when it gets cold you can shut the door.

The preservatives were down in the cellar. I would eat ate her preservatives. I was hungry. I was just playing around and nobody was in there. She went out. In the summertime, everybody went out and I was the only person in the house, by myself, and I got into her preservatives. And I ate about a whole jar, our peaches, our applesauce. And a pot of spaghetties. And I ate flour, ate five pounds of sugar, syrup, drunk the syrup, I ate white sugar — just ate it all up.

I took a loaf of bread upstairs, and I would be hiding it. Whole loaf of bread. And my mother would be looking for the loaf of bread and ax the girls, "Did you see the loaf of bread, that I bought?" Nope, nobody knew. And every time she would clean, do her Christmas cleanin', there was bread hidden in the closet in the back room. And she axed the girls, "How did all this bread get in here?" And I would be taking bread, eating bread piece by piece. I would feel like I was hungry. And the girls said, "No, I don't know how that got in there." She said, "Maybe that Roland Johnson, maybe that boy did it again." Yep. She could never keep a loaf of bread or anything. She'd try to hide it; she'd put it away, put it up — I'd still get it. Couldn't understand why I eat so much.

And my father came home and my father said, "Just leave that boy alone; he's just sick." He didn't whop me too much, he whop all the rest of them, but he didn't touch me at all. And my mother said, "If your father would have whop you, maybe things would have changed better." Because he can come down, he can hit you hard, and whip you. I don't know why he didn't whop me. I guess he just said, "Well, he's just sick."

My parents would send me down to the store and I would be coming back with a pocket full of stuff. We had a ice cream store. My father would send me to get razors. And every time I come in I would go out with a pop. They wouldn't let me come in. She'd look up at the mirror that be in front of the store — "Don't come in here." They'd be watching me like a dog.

There was my brother-in-law, Tom Rivers, and he used to work down at the store. It was down the street. There was kids playing outside when I went out. They was playing rope, the girls. And boys was playing with the wagons and with the toys. I wasn't paying too much attention. Every time my mother would send me to the store, he knew that I as the one who come into the store and pick up everything without paying for it. He would watch. But he never said nothing to the storekeeper. The store manager thought that the people that worked in the store would be lifting up stuff without paying for it. Every time my mother send me to the store I would come back home with a pocket full of jellybeans, and pies and cakes. I guess later down the line he went and told Joe, the storekeeper that we had a person that come in here and picked up something and they would walk out and his pockets would be loaded. And he would laugh. He would sit there and laugh, not Joe, but my brother-in-law. I brought back the milk, but the time I paid for the milk, my pockets, both pockets was loaded. Coat pocket, pants pocket, was loaded full of jellybeans and cake and pies and whatever I could get my hands on. Every time she would go down to Joe's store, he told my mother, "You know your son, he comes in here, he would pay for the milk and pay for the loaf of bread, but he doesn't pay for the stuff that he take off my shelf." So my mother found out. She didn't whip me at that time, but she told the storekeeper, "I know, I know, I know him — you don't have to tell me — I'll get him." I guess she paid for the stuff that I took, but the guy was so nice; she knew him for thirteen years. This was up in North Philly, on Cleveland Street.

And Tom Rivers would laugh, 'cause when he came at my house and my mother would put a plate out for my oldest brother when he come home from work, I would be in sneaking in the kitchen, taking his plate, and eat it. I think it was a piece of chicken on the plate and I would be the one who quickly took his plate and ate it. I just took the chicken off the plate and ate it. And William axed Mom, William would say, "Mom, there's nothing on this plate. Didn't you put a plate down for me?" "Well, is it there?" He just said, "No. It's not here." And Tom would die laughing. And my sister, Madeleine, said, "What are you laughing about?" And he wouldn't say anything; he would just laugh. They was probably dating then.

Well, I got fat.

I was like, rolled up, just fat. My neck was this way and my stomach was out that way. I was just huffin' and puffin' and trying to walk.

And that was the time that I would be eating a whole lot of ice cream too. A gallon full of ice cream. My stomach would be poked out. Fat. From the time that I was small I was looking for food, more food. My mother just could not figure out why was he eating so much. "Why is he eating all this sugar and stuff. Why doesn't he have sugar diabetes by now?" I was just blowed up and she just couldn't find the reason for it. I think I gave my mother more trouble ... They took me to a doctor. And they took me to a hospital. The doctors says, "Well, we'll keep him here in the hospital, we'll see how he does in the hospital, and see makes him eat so much." So they gave me all this food, and I would eat. Plate would be piled up this high and I would eat, eat, eat, eat. Until, til my stomach got busted, fatter, stretched out. I would eat, see, and the doctor would say, "Hmph. I don't know where he put it all. I don't know where he put it all." They took blood testses; they took everything that they could take: X-rays, eating disorder tests. I guess they was just testing me out to see how much food I could eat. I ate the whole plate. 'Much food that they put in front of me. Even the nurses could not figure out why he ate so much: "We gave him all this food, and he still want ... " — I still wanted more. They said to my mother, "Mrs. Johnson, we put everything in front of him to see why he eats so much; we could not find a way why he eats so much. There's nothing wrong with him." They just said, "Mrs. Johnson, your son is just a big eater."

And the doctor said he's a mental retard — retardation. That's where they got that from. I was outside the hall. I found it out from my mother. But she didn't know what it meant.

And when I came out of the hospital in the summer, when she brought me home, my stomach was out like ... I couldn't fit through the door. And the neighbor says — he was looking, they was all looking outside — "Mrs. Johnson, is that your son? Who's that boy who's running in front of you? Who's that little boy, running next to you? No, come on, that's not your son."

And she said, "Yep, that's him, that's that old big eater." And the neighbor said, "Hmm, he kind of put a little weight on himself — a big weight." And then my mother said, "Hmph. I still don't know what to do with him. The doctors can't find out what's wrong with you. Don't know."

I was felt like I did not get enough to eat. I was always eating, eating, eating all the time. If it wasn't the preservative, if it wasn't something ... I ate a piece of fat. My sister sent me out to empty the garbage can and I took the fat out of the garbage can and ate it with coffee grounds on it — I just I ate it. I just couldn't understand why it made me eat so much.

She made good meals; it was enough food there for everybody; it was enough. She made some fried fish — my father was crazy over fish — and stew and roast beef, pork chops — 'cause he always liked pork chops — and roast beef and mashed potatoes. Spaghetties, beans. I liked her black-eyed peas. Corn bread. She made it from scratch. Cake, apple pies, sweet potato pies. She didn't have the girls helping her. She just did it all herself. She did all the cooking herself. Of course she was young at that time.

I don't think she meant it to do it to spite me, I think that she wanted to do it just to make me understand that you don't do things like that. She burned me, like. I don't think she meant to do that, but at that time she didn't know how to handle me. She turned on the stove — it was a gas stove — and she lay that knife down. Then she put it on my hand and burnt me with it. And then she had an iron and she whipped me with the iron cord and made bruises all over my back. I don't blame her for it — I probably needed it, a licking. She gave me a good licking, the licking of my life. She really beat me.

My mother tried. She couldn't take it anymore. I was the last child; this was very painful for her. She was just ... My father

22

was just trying to find out where to do with this boy. Because nobody couldn't tell her what to do with me. There was no social workers back in them days or case managers. She just said, "Well, Roy, you gotta help me think of something, where to put this boy, because I can't take it no more."

I had an aunt and uncle and they came over and they said, "What are you feeding Roland?" My mama said, "I'm not feeding him anything. He's just grabbing up the food." And my aunt said, "I have a son that way too." She's on my mother's side; she had a son that ate the same thing like I used to do. His name is Herbie Thomas. He used to do the same thing that I used to do. He ran away from home, walked out the door and never come back. She couldn't do nothing with him.

I think it was after New Year's that fire happened, that I was playing with the matches. It was cold; it was ten below. I was on the second floor and my mother bought me a big fire truck and I was playing with this, just playing around, and I got a-hold of some matches, and the matches got on fire. And all this — flames — started shooting up. The back bedroom was on fire. It was very, very painful, when you seen this fire and flames shooting up. And they called my sister, "Well, you'd better go see what that boy is doing upstairs!" And they came up, and they saw this fire. And they pulled me, get me out of the room they did. And the fire truck come. I remember the next-door neighbors said they saw the smoke coming up out of the roof and almost through their house. My sister tried to put the fire out; she threw some water on the fire. She almost had the fire out. And the fire truck came, and they said we had to make sure that fire was out. The fire truck had had to put it out with the hose. She got a new box spring for some of us to sleep in and that's the box spring that got on fire.

So she taught me a lesson, not to be playing with matches. She said, "You want to play with matches? Oh! Hold your hands out. I'll show you how to play with matches." So she burned me. She burned me with a knife. And she locked me in the shed kitchen.

My mother said, "Well, I can't do nothing with him. I try. Very hard." At that time there was nobody around to talk to, to help my mother with that.

And my mother really got on me too. It was hot and my Aunt Mabel and Aunt Hazel and Aunt Pearl — that's my mother's sisters — was sitting around the table. All I remember for my birthday I was locked up in the shed kitchen. They would come and see my mother, all of her sisters, used to come and see my mother and they would talk. And they says to my mother, "You know something, you need to put that boy away. You need to put him away somewhere. If you can't handle him, he needs to be put away somewhere." I think she tried to work out the things for herself. She took me to police, but they just couldn't find the reason. It was just a habit that I had. She said that, "You will have to be put away somewhere;" that, "I can't handle you no more." And that's all she said. I was making things harder for her. So she went and axed and somebody said, "Well, the only thing we can do for you, Mrs. Johnson — see if you can take him to court and see what they can do for you." And she took me to court.

I went to court lots of times. I was in and out of courts. She wanted to know how to deal with me; she wanted to know how can she work with me — because she had her hands full. So they took me to a child court in Philadelphia somewhere. All I remember is seeing a lot of big policemen, and a big judge and she had to get on the stand and tell the judge what was going on.

I was afraid. I didn't know what they was going to do to me. They questioned me: "Did you know the things that you do? Did you understand why you're here?"

And I said no.

They axed me some other questions and I just didn't know.

And the judge told my mother, I guess, to keep an eye on me. But I think it got too much for her. I mean, she just couldn't; her hands was just tied, fulled up — with my father working and she's trying to struggle with the kids, with me, and it was just kind of hard to do that.

And then the last time they came up with the decision that, "He should went to Pennhurst."

I think they send my mother a letter and said that, "We have found a place for your son. Either choose one of the three institutions." Either the first one was Embreeville State Hospital and the second one was Byberry State Hospital and the third one was Pennhurst. It was a decision for her to make, not me — at that time I was small, so she made the decision. My father helped to make the decision. And that's the only one she picked out.

I didn't know at the time what was Pennhurst. I heard of it. All I knew about it was it was an institution, a place for a person that has some kind of problems, that they would try and deal with. It scared me a little. I thought about: "This is it; this is it for me. I guess I will be locked up in there, in a big cellar, in a big basement with locks — a jail with paddle-locks on it."

My father was working; my mother was home. I think it was some people from the state drove me and my mother out to Pennhurst. I was in the car and my mother was in the car and we went up to Pennhurst. I was put away at Pennhurst State School in 1958.

Roland on the grounds of the
Pennhurst State School and Hospital

PENNHURST

· ·

Aﬕter that long ride up there, it was just horrible. That was
very scary. Very, very frightening. I was crying that I would
never see them again, my family or sister. We went out into this
great big institution that I didn't know anything about.

I saw Pennhurst for the first time. Where you come down on
the main road you see this big thing up at Pennhurst, the water
tower, coming in to Pennhurst. Things looked different to me —
because it wasn't like a house that I lived in. I'm out here in this
gray institution with three thousand people that live in it. It was
just something that I didn't like. They had a playground there as
you come to a dead end. And the office.

They admit me on the hospital ward. It looked to me it was
all right. I was on the hospital ward before they discharge you
from the hospital and put you on the ward. It looked pretty
good to me. They fed me very good, filled my plate up with a
lot of food. It smelled like a hospital, like a regular hospital; it
didn't smell like it had a strong odor. It had beds, lots of beds
and lots of nurses and different wards for the little kids and for
older people. And cribs that had babies that was sent there at
Pennhurst. I didn't know first thing about the place; didn't know
where I was going or what I was doing there. But I knew what I
was sent there for — to be out of my mother's head.

Well, I was on the hospital ward. They interview your mother
— my mother — and they axed my mother some questions. I
wasn't there; I was getting undressed to be on the ward. I didn't
know what she was saying; I don't know what took place. All I

29

knew — they took me back in the hospital ward and my mother was talking to Mrs. Clark.

But once I was there things got very overwhelmed to me. I stayed there for a week and ten days. They did some tests, psychological evaleration and stuff like that. The doctor keep axing questions. It was so much overwhelming that there's this great big ward with all these people; I'm used to my mother and father, my sisters. Never was used to all these other people around. It was just something. I was just crying, with tears. I cried that, "My mommy's gone; my daddy's gone. I will never see my sisters again or my brother or anybody. I'm here for life."

I thought that, "Here I am. I'm here and there's nothing that nobody can do. Nobody can do anything about it. I put myself there; I got myself into all this mischief and trouble and that's why I was here, to try to better myself." Maybe I had a lot of guilt in me. And that's why I was sent there. I had a lot of bad memories — things that I used to do, things I used to take. And if I didn't take them, I would be still living with my mother instead of at Pennhurst. If I wish back, if I wished that I could do it over again, maybe that possibility that I wouldn't have control over myself, that I might have to do it all over again, stealing and taking things and eating my mother out of the house ... I guess it was just a thing that I could not think of ... I put a thing down back in my memories: I would not do that anymore; if I came out of Pennhurst, I would not do it, not eat my mother out of the house anymore ; I'd change.

I cried when my mother left; I cried before she left and after she left. And I cried when I left out — when they transferred me to the ward, to D-4.

• • •

It was very high function ward. All different patie:
colored, all mixed. No women — women's used to
the hill. And the boys'd be on the boys' side, down the hill.
It was about a hundred people on the ward. All the beds on
one side; there was a bedroom on that side, bedroom on that
side, windows in the middle — attendants' windows — the staff
offices in between the bedrooms.

Everybody had a locker; the attendant had a key to open up the
lockers; nobody could have their own keys. Attendants would
mark the clothes with your name in it, so when they sent the
clothes out to the laundry they know this is your clothes, they're
nobody else's clothes. Anything that you get for Christmas they
would lock 'em up in the locker.

In the day room they had a TV; that's all that was there — just
TV and bench. No toys. Only toys in school.

It sounded like vibrations: crazy people was going out of their
heads, out of their wits. It just sound like people that need to
belong there. It sound to me, in my personal feeling, that people
was just doing things that should not have happened. So that's
what it sound like; it sounded like — fear; that something not
right. It was just scary — a frightened, scary place.

The floor was waxed and polished every day and they would
run to move all the benches and mop the floors and strip the
floor and lay new wax down. And we would help to move the
benches back in the day room after the floor's been waxed. They
would take the machine and go over it and polish the floor and
the bedrooms.

I used to stand in line, waiting for a toothbrush. They had
green and striped clothes — state clothes. We used to get shoes
from Graterford Prison. I was afraid that somebody would steal

some good personal things that I had, that they would just take that out of under my nose.

I went around with groups. We had to go outside or we went down across the subway. The subway was underground; we would walk thru there when it snowed, rained. We would walk through underground, the subway, to the dining room. It was a big, big subway; it was hard for me to figure it out; all the buildings was connected.

They had a dairy. The truck used to come early in the morning to pick up the milk and have it homogenized. I saw it around six o'clock when I was going over to the dining room. It would stop at the kitchen and they would pick up something from there. Trucks would bring coal; they would wave [weigh — K.W.] it before they take it down there to the powerhouse, the generator with all the steam.

I was afraid of these grown men — these was not workers; these was actually patients on the ward. We would be sitting on the long benches after we come in from the dining room hall or come home after school; we would come back and we would be watching TV. We had a black and white; we didn't have a colored one. I used to watch *The American Bandstand* after school. And I seen these people doing things to these other children and I say, "I hope this don't happen to me." And I just was scared; I was frightened.

I believe that the workers had their hands tied. It was only three attendants on the ward at that time; there was be about a hundred and twenty-two patients. The attendants had their hands full. They was overloaded with work, taking care of the residents and making sure the residents get the places where they're supposed to go.

It was just a terrible thing to see. The doctors would make the rounds on the ward and the nurses too. And the supervisor would make the rounds, but this didn't take place until when the other shifts was changing over.

I didn't like it at all. Boys used to call me names and laugh at me. It was some of my age, but not much. People would be following you around and axing you for things and stuff like that.

I got scared at around the nighttime. All this stuff happened late at night. Lot of people was sleeping. And they'd be boys with these grown people and they would be waking up other people, their friends, getting them out of bed. I thought that they was going to do that to me. And they did and I couldn't do nothing about it.

At that time I was sexual abused.

It was very bad. Grown people laid me down on the floor and nowhere to break away from them and tell them, "No, you can't do this."

It was grown patients, higher functioning patients. They had sexual with little kids. And no one would help. This would all happen when the attendants wasn't looking. Some of the attendants was sleeping, wasn't aware of what's going on. And they would have sex with me. And they did all kinds of things to me. They did awful things to me. It was very scary. It was very, very painful.

• • •

My family didn't visit, not right away. I was ashamed of people using me when I was a little boy. I don't know ... It was just very hard to talk about. I tried to talk to my father about it,

33

but he was very busy; I just couldn't talk to him. I did try tell my mother, but I don't think she could do much about it. She would tell me, "If they bother you again, you just tell somebody. Go and tell somebody." And every time I tell somebody, they do the same thing over after the attendants leave. She talked to the supervisor when she came to visit me: "I heard there's some problems with my son ... " and "Could you help him? He tells me that boys is picking on him and doing things with him." The supervisor didn't do anything. They talked to my mother that that didn't happen.

It did happen.

But I wasn't disappointed; I can pick up things when not even looking; I can feel something. I pick up scents [sense? — K.W.] — like someone is coming towards me or something, getting ready to hit me or something — I can pick up a scent. My mother wasn't a person that would know anybody that she could go to; she had no control over that.

My first teacher treated us nice. That's how I remember. There was lots of kids, lots of boys and girls. We used to work on how to learn to write our letters, ABC's, and how to spell, how to print, write your name and stuff like that; sing songs — "The wipers on the bus goes 'swish, swish, swish' ... Tic, tac, toe ... When the leaves turn colors in the autumn, red, orange, gold, and brown ... "

I went to homemaking, and sewing, and cooking. They teached us how to bake a cake and pies. I learned about wood shop: I made tables, coffee tables, bird houses, a wagon, a child's desk table, stuff like that. We'd sew pants; I made a dress, a shirt.

Some would go in at ten o'clock; some would go at one o'clock. I was protected from school, because people was around. They

34

would not go to hit me and stuff like that.

I had a friend. He used to get me scared. He used to say, "If you don't watch yourself here, they will write a little note and send you to a bad ward, and they will keep you on the ward and put you in the sweat box, put you in shackles and restraint jackets ... " and all this kind of stuff.

I said, "Ah, c'mon. Don't tell me that;" I said, "C'mon, you're not frightening ... "

He said, "Yep, that's what they'll do. If you don't listen, that's what they'll do."

I said, "No, it's not true."

He was right.

There was people on the punishment ward all the time. They would be writing conduct reports and they would be sent to the punishment ward.

I was on punishment wards M-1, U-2, K-1, V-2, K-2, I-2. The numbers had to do with what floor the unit was on ... physical handicaps — they couldn't feed themself, they couldn't go to the bathroom themself, they couldn't bathe themself, they couldn't move anywhere ...

That didn't happen right away. It took me til I got used to it — Pennhurst. And that's when people would get me upset and call me names — "You're stupid. You're crazy" and all that kind of stuff. Patients would say that. I don't know what they would say that to me for; I had no idea. It didn't make me feel good. That make me mad because they would call me like "Dummy ... Dopey ... Don't know nothing ... " — and so I got mad. I tried to tell somebody to make them stop, but they wouldn't make them stop. And I got upset and I cracked one of the windows out. They punished me on the ward for breaking the window. I was a person that had to be always breaking up windows when I would get upset. It was people bothering me, calling names. "You'll never learn; you're crazy; you're an idiot; you're stupid! You don't need to be on this ward; you need to be put on some other ward." So I would just bust out windows.

So they would write up conduct reports and put me on a punishment ward — just lock me up in there and make me scrub down walls for a week; doing all kinds of things — scrubbing soiled benches.

The reason why that it was locked, they had low-grades, that they would not get out. They had one college for the low-grade ... They had different colleges [cottages — K.W.], different wards for different ... They had wards for the bright ones and then they wards for the lower ones.

That's the words that they was mentioned at Pennhurst, so that's the word that I have to use. They don't say them anymore because they're outside now, they're out in the community; they don't hear them words any more.

If you had spent your time up there, you wouldn't like it. You wouldn't like it. If you was in my shoe, you would cry.

The low-grade ward: It was filthy and dirty — holes in the walls, holes in the floor. Walls would be cracking open; clients would eat the paste, the chalk off the wall, the tile off the wall. They would just eat it. And the only way to keep them from eating it would be put them in restraints, tie them to the benches. And that's what I seen one day.

To tell you the truth, Pennhurst smelled like a doghouse. It just smell like feces. Rats crawling, roaches crawling all over; this was on the low-grade wards. Holes in the wall, big holes in the floors. It was awful to see. You would cry to see people living in that kind of filth. Horrible. Feces and pee on the floor, flies coming in the windows. It was a lot of wards with lower function — the C functions, they used to call 'em. I don't know what that is, but it's something to do their mobility; they can't address themselves. The real, real low.

I remember they'd call me screwballs and retarded and stuff like that: "What are you doing here, you retarded person. You look scary." And I got very, very, very angry and crashed out, windows. I got beated with mop handles. I had to scrub beds for punishment.

• • •

It wasn't all bad. We went to church — a yellow bus took us out, the choir, to sing at another church. They had a gymnasium; they would ax the choir to come and surrender a selection of church singing. I would go along with them. I didn't sing with the choir, but I used to help Reverend Yost lighting candles on the altar (they really call them altar boys) — he put me on the list to go. I was proud about getting on the bus and going to church. He showed religion movies in the summer. And then I would light the candles for the Protestant church on Sunday afternoon. The Catholics would have church in the morning and we would have church in the afternoon. I used to set up the rooms at the school building. Sister Bernadette used to come, the Catholic sister, and have classes every Tuesday. We had — the Protestants had — a Bible School down on one of the wards.

I was in Boy Scouts. And then we used to play up there at Royersford and Spring City and Pottstown when I was a Boy Scout. We used to march. Our Boy Scout uniform would be Troop 91.

They had a band for Labor Day and May Day and they had a May Queen. This was fun: we would get dressed up on whatever day that May Day would fall on; somebody would be dressed as the May Queen — one of the girls, with a crown — and we would dance around the Maypole. And then we would have tumblers — we would dress in white uniforms — white pants, white shirts — and we would tumble. That was fun to do. Mrs. Moyer, that's the principal, she would have a big box up in the attic and every year after May Day was over we would have to put all our clothes up in the big box in the attic.

There was a baseball league from the different wards. Dave Miller would make up schedules; he was head of the recreation department. We won some championships. Trophies about this high would sit over in the administration building. We had no access to it. They'd just sit in there. I hit a home run.

They used to show movies every Friday on a big projector in the auditorium. When you come down over the hill on the boys' side, there would be a big gym room and the auditorium. That's where the Catholics had their church in the morning and the Protestants had their church in the afternoon. And that's where during the weekdays we had gym. It was a big auditorium; they had a great big, wide, electric movie screen and a real movie projector. We would get the movies, 'cause I used to work in the storeroom area. They would bring the movie reels in on a truck from Philadelphia. There was no popcorn — there was nowhere they could make popcorn there.

Everybody had a joke for each other. We was just laughing about jokes and making jokes. It was always funny. There was just things that people laugh about. It was just a joke that would say, "Oh, there's that so-and-so person. Look at that person walking silly!" They wasn't really acting silly. It was just cracking jokes. I mean that the higher function was making jokes. It was always funny. But it didn't help me to get out of there. All I remember, that there was a lot of people that I knew, up there, way back ago. Many many years ago.

We used to play checkers and we used to play records and have a dance at the gym and every Christmas a party. The lower functions would go first and then the higher functions would go last. They would have Halloween parties — I dressed up as a nurse for Halloween. A big Thanksgiving dinner for everybody.

They had swings down on the playground and every time it would snow we used to go sledding. They would put a rope on the truck and pull us up the hill. Yeah, I had a lot of fun.

They had ice-skating. I never ice skate — I'm not going to break my legs. They used to teach us to roller skate in gym; you used to get a chair and roller around the auditorium. I fell down sometimes, but they'd put a chair in front of me, and I used to push the chair going on around the floor and I learned that way how to skate. Once a month we would go up on a yellow bus to Pottstown to Ringing Rocks, skating. That was fun; that was very fun, skating.

And then I had a penpal buddy. He used to write me a letter every other month. I found somebody to read it to me — my schoolteacher. I never know the person's name; it had their address on it, but I didn't know where they lived. In the letter it said, "Dear Roland, I hope that you are feeling fine today. I am writing to see how you are doing. I know that life is not too cool for you, but I hope that you will get out some day. And I'm sending you ... " They would be sending me cards — birthday cards and stuff. They used to send me a Christmas package. I didn't know where it came from. It didn't come from my mother; it didn't come from my father. And I would get an Easter card and they would send Easter eggs.

We used to have Easter egg hunts. We had picnics in different months — a Memorial Day picnic and a Fourth of July picnic and a Labor Day picnic on the grounds. Some families came, I remember. We got on the Spring City fire truck, the one that squirts water and people would get wet. It was very nice. They drove us around on hayrides. We had an open house every May.

At Christmas someone would get dressed up as Santa Claus and go to the low-grades wards and give out candy and sing Christmas carols. I know, I was punish on one of the wards.

I was punished on the ward and I seen what other patients had to go through. And they had to lie about it. That when their parents would come to see them staff would say, "Well, we didn't do that."

Staff would tell you, "And if you go and tell your parents that we did it, we will find out and we will write a little note and put you on another ward." And they'll put you in a hole, a sweat box. And they would beat you up there, if you told your parents that this was happening. I was so frightened.

And not only just me. There was other clients being abused, getting hit over with the mop. And this is not patients doing this. This is staff. I saw it with my own very eyes.

But I didn't get hit with a broomstick, a broom handle. It was other people got hit. Patients would get hit. These was patients that could not take care of themselves, they couldn't talk for themselves, they was like low function — they would get hit. I don't know why. Don't ax me — I don't know what in the world they would hit them up for, the reason.

40

So, I pretty nervous, being on a punishment ward. That's wh... I thought that things wasn't right for me. I was very scared, very frightened, very like — suicidal. Why I was there at Pennhurst? I was going suicidal of myself; take my life. But something said, "You don't want to do that; you got a lot to offer." And I didn't. So I had a lot of frightened, scary moments.

I was bad; I had my bad behaviors up there too. There was some things that I used to do, like striking at the attendants, hitting back at the attendants. I used to. They would make me upset. I would smash a window.

Dr. P. used to suture me up when I bust out the windows; he used to put sutures in me; he was really strict. Somebody got me upset. Think it's this wrist. The right. The mark's not there now. They would suture my wrists, 'cause if they didn't suture that I would bleed to death. I would just smash the window; it would cut my wrists. I remember that every time I used to be punished for something, being on a low-grade ward, cleaning up soil; patient feces and stuff.

I would say I'm a person that was lost and lonely and just in a desert world. And no one to talk to. Just out there in a big institution all by myself. All lonely. That's how I'd 'scribe it. I thought I would be there forever. I was kinda thinking that on that issue — that I would be there, if I didn't stop doing the things that I used to do, I would be there for a long time.

• • •

My mother used to come and visit me when the car was working; if the car was broke she couldn't come. She would write letters to me; one of the teachers at school used to read me the letters. My sisters came — Laverne came, Bertha May came, Bootsie came. I would spend a pretty good day with them, a whole day, just walk around on the grounds and go to the canteen. We would be having a conversation, just walking around.

My mother said she couldn't believe how skinny I got. I was real thin. "Boy, you amaze me," she says. I went home 'round Christmas and Easter every year. And that would make me feel good. I would stay a couple weeks. My mother said that, "Gee, you talk almost like a white person. Where you get all this 'Thank you' and 'No, thank you' and stuff like that. Boy, they must have taught you something." I tried to tell them what it was like, when I came home for a home visit. But it was horrible to talk about. It was a horrible place, very horrible. I couldn't talk too much anymore. It was hard, but I had to go back, finish out my sentence, until they tell me I could go.

In the summertime I saw this young boy get thrown out the window. I saw it 'cause I was in the day room. On some of these low-grade wards they had these kind of screens that you can't push out, that you lock with a key. Now this was on a bright ward; they didn't have screens in the window. It happened like three to eleven shift; the staff was coming on — the change of staff; the attendant was doing something. This other person threw him out the window, pushed the person outside the window, all the way out, when the attendants was not looking. I saw that happened. I didn't think that boy would live. There was a solid, a hard solid ground where this person got thrown out the window — broke his leg and broke his hip. I think that it was just an awful sight to see. I cried 'bout it. We went and told the attendant — but what more did they do; the damage happened. And they rushed him up into the hospital, got his leg in a cast, and put him in a traction: they put your legs up in the air with rope.

Anybody was bad, if anybody got caught doing something, they get put on a punishment ward and they would stay there til the end of their punishment, for a week, maybe two weeks. I was on the worst punishment ward and I had to do the scrubbing: scrub the benches and scrub cribs and scrub the walls down.

It was horrible. I saw people get knocked — just hitting them with brooms and mop handles. Their heads would be cut open; they would send them to the hospital with their heads split open; blood would be bleeding; mouth would be all swollen up. And I cried; I really did — because they couldn't fight for themself. It was horrible.

I wonder why did this go on, why did kept happening? And from the time that I was up there, it still went on; things didn't change any.

Where I was living they would be hitting too — them big strong boys. It wasn't the attendants that did it; it was the patients: Charles R., Eddie T., and Eddie S., and other people. They would hit them over the head with mop handles and brooms — whatever they could get their hands on; they would hit them. I never got hit; I got out of that; I hid in the bedroom underneath all the beds down in the rows. They chasing everybody else around; they couldn't catch me. I was very scared. They hit everybody else but they couldn't get me.

They would be going to the hospital with cut heads and sores on the backs and Dr. W. would come around: "What's all these patients being hit for?" And Dr. W. would write out prescriptions for nerve relaxers and Thorazines and stuff like that. The medicine cabinet would be open — they would have medicine cabinets open, wide open — and somebody got themselves a bottle of Thorazines, liquid Thorazine, and drunk a whole bottle and got very sick and they put him in the hospital — they was trying to pump the stuff out of him — and he died the next day. Lord knows where the attendants was at.

• • •

Shorty McVeigh knew what was going on. He knew. But there's only so much that he could do. He used to like me a lot; he used to take me around to make rounds with him. I think I was his favorite. Not that it was favoritism — he had another person that used to go off, get upset, and he used to take him around too on the wards, so that would kind of help him a little and after a while he got used to it and he kept kind of quiet.

Well, I was tired of going on punishment wards, scrubbing cribs and cleaning up mildew and scrubbing benches and stuff. I used to just scrub cribs all day. I got tired of it.

But Shorty McVeigh used to take me around on the wards every time he would make the rounds. He said, "If you don't stop doing this, you will never get out of here. You will always be on punishment wards." He said that, "Your behavior wasn't too cool." I listened.

Yeah, Shorty McVeigh was like a companion, a friend, that I could talk to, that could understand things about a person; he could really seek out things — what was going on. He was a supervisor. He'd sit down and talk with me, talk about different things, things you should not do, things you should not have done.

"You should not go on a punishment ward. You're too smart for that. Don't make me put you on a punishment ward."

Well, it learned to me this was my doing; this was my behavior; that I was placed in there just to show me to stop; to cut out my behavior. Shorty ... Shorty McVeigh. I liked that. I was acting like a child. Shorty McVeigh helped me with this.

And I stopped it. He coaxed me and said, "That's not nice, to break windows and do things like that. You doing harm to yourself, instead of helping yourself to get better." So he talked to me and tried to encourage me; he took me around in the wards with him while he was making rounds. And I stopped.

It took me a long time. I was trying to avoid things when I was there. But it's kinda hard to avoid things, because you hear a lots of things. You try not to let it bother you, but sometimes in the inside of you it builds up anxiety; that tension builds up, that you want to go after somebody. They're saying things to you or about you; they're doing that. But all the time Shorty McVeigh would say, "You can't do that. Don't do it. It's not worth it. You'll get punished for it. It's not worth it. Just let it go."

It took for a while — months and months and months; years and years — till it changed; till I said, "This is it. I'm tired of it." So then I behaved myself and didn't do it no more. I decided myself.

I remember we had a very big snowstorm and Shorty McVeigh used to made us go out and shovel snow, make the paths. "Well, maybe I'll take you for a ride in the car somewhere." That's what he used to do. He would take me to his house and show me his big garden. He had a nice garden up there; he didn't live too far from Pennhurst. He showed me around and he brought me back.

At the time he passed, I did not go to his funeral because things was very upsetting to me. There was other people, other patients, that went to his funeral. But I didn't go. I could've gone; I decided not to.

Well, I stopped being afraid as I got older. Things was looking up for me, that I was going out and going home and getting out of Pennhurst and being with my mother. And all of a sudden it just stopped — just like that.

I used to go to the dentist; the routine was like once a year; they cleaned my teeth and I had a lot of cavities filled. And I had teeth broked — cracked. That happened in the patients' cafeteria. One of the persons threw a stool because he was upset and cracked my tooth. He wasn't upset at me; he was just upset in general. And I had to go to the dentist.

I had nosebleeds that would just start; I went to the 'spenser to make it stop. And I remember fighting. A little boy would always call me names — knucklehead — and I would call him stupid. That boy beat me up; I beat him up. My lip got cut and they had to suture it up. I told them I fell down steps, so I won't have to go on the punishment.

I had a very bad cold, very bad cold, I hadda be admitted in the hospital. I had chest X-rays; I had a fever, a cold or something in the lungs.

And my ears would be ringing, just be ringing. I don't know what for. The doctors say there's nothing you can do about that. They still ring.

They used to spray people with bug juice — what's it called — wintergreen, for the little bugs that crawls around — lice. They spray you for it. We stand in long lines and they sprayed us in the locker room. They put it on your penis. And you had to suffer with it. And that stuff burnt. That's what they did. And then we all had to take a shower after they sprayed. And then anybody got caught doing anything would get more punishment.

Shorty McVeigh's wife used to work at the laboratory. She was the vampire! (I didn't call her that.) She used to take blood and then she used to work at the morgue room. She knew me. She used to draw blood from me all the time. She would take the blood all the time because I had gonorrhea, syphilis. It was from other boys having sex with me. They kept me on the hospital ward about six weeks on penicillin, til I got rid of it. It was a couple times. Those boys wanted me to have sex with them. Eddie T. the most; he got caught messing around with some girl, a crippled girl, and the parents sued Pennhurst. Eddie T. tried to help her out of the chair so she could have sex with him; broke the inside her, her vagina, and they sent him to court for doing that. He had to go to jail; I don't know what happened after that; we didn't see him no more.

I had a friend, long time ago, but he got killed. He got killed on a second-floor landing.

He was a good friend of mine and we used to talk about the good old days. Back way, way back before — he would tell me about things happening way back ago, before I came. He used to talk about Mr. William P., the superintendent. He was the bad guy. He would send people to the punishment wards and they got hit over the head with clubs, with bats, and broom handles; he didn't care. He was long gone when I heard about it. It used to be rough up there. Yeah, he was a friend of mine. Me and him used to go up to Pottstown together. And something happened and he got killed. This friend of mine got hanged, he was tied up and hanged. They found the rope around his neck. They used him; he was abused, sexual abused. They tied him up, with his hands down, back of his arms, his feet all tied up, a mouth gag. He tried to holler for help. Nobody really came to his rescue. And next day he was dead — the rope was so tight, they couldn't revive him. I don't know from the day how it happened.

It was not an attendant; it was probably one of the patients up there.

They found him the next evening, found him dead. Twenty-four hours the man was dead, deceased. And nobody knew about it until a nurse made her rounds down on each floor and came up on that deceased, dead man.

Mrs. B. came above us and she said, "I smell something strange." She went down on the back fire escapes. And so they found that body.

And that's when they did the investigating of Pennhurst. That's when they took a very serious look at that. That's when first came open up the case about Pennhurst. And I think that is a very helpful thing that they did to try to move, to look into that direction, and to try to fill that gap to look to see what can be done.

They had the State Police in up there. They talked with other residents. I didn't see it, but I heard it. They didn't talk to me, 'cause I was working in the 'tendants' cafeteria.

Then Dr. Potkonski came along, Leopold Potkonski. He kind of changed things. He knew what was going on, because he worked down at Norristown State Hospital. He was the Superintendent down there. He kind of tried to phase out people that was doing these things. But it still kept going on. It still happened. It was no change. He was just probably one person to do, to handle the whole loads of these places. But it's kind of silly to come with these places, to be institutionalized. I believe that I don't feel like no one should be even in an institution.

• • •

I remember the first ward that I worked on. I was about seventeen or eighteen. It was snowing; they had a few staff persons on M-1, but they didn't have enough staff persons to cover that

48

ward. When it was cold and snow they didn't have staff — one of the staff had to work overtime; they couldn't get another staff to change shift. And we had to sleep there when there was no staff. I remember he said that, "Roland is my workboy this week." There'd be eight or seven people worked on a ward, but we never got paid fot it. The staff person just watched, just watched, the head staff person. Patients used to do all the work. They helped to change the babies. So we had to bathe them and wash them and brush their teeth and stuff like that. Now these are people that could not able to take care of themselves. These people who had low-grades used to wet the floors and I had to clean them up; I had to get in the showers with them and give them baths. Somebody had to do it. I would get in the shower; they might even be messing on themselves. I felt sorry for them; they couldn't help themselves. That's the first job that I had at Pennhurst.

And then they placed me somewhere else. From M-1 I used to work at the U-2, helping feed patients up there. The trucks would come around, the food trucks, to every ward except the bright boys, to all the low-grade wards. The patients that used to work in the dining room, they used to take the food trucks out; filled them up with soup and mashed potatoes — whatever they had.

There was people I used to take care of, lot of people; I don't know their names, but I had my hands full. It was a nice thing to do. That felt like you're helping somebody else that they can't not be helped. I was pleased to do that. People could not feed themselves.

Whatever they need me to do: when they was short, I helped. I used to feed the babies. I used to work up on the hospital ward. They had little babies with big heads; one child, one guy, one fellow had a big head; he couldn't move; we had to turn his head over, turn him sideways — so he wouldn't get sores on his back — and change diapers, change the sheets, and feed them with a spoon. It was pretty hard to feed 'em. But we fed 'em. They was laying down; some of 'em could sit up, and some of 'em couldn't.

I saw a patient got burnt in the hot water in the tub during the day all over his body. The water was hot and they didn't do the temperature. They had the doctors look at him and they sent him over to the dispenser. And they put some salve on him and bandages. It was terrible. And somebody died. I remember they rolled the person out in the hallway and the doctor pronounced them dead.

I worked in the barber shop; they showed me how to use the 'lectric clippers. I was going around the colleges cutting hair, shaving patients' faces — those who couldn't shave themself. I had a apron and a shirt and a pocket where you put the comb and scissors. They would have the razors on the ward. I had to hold people, lower function ones who couldn't keep still. Not all, but some of them just couldn't keep their hair combed; we cut their hair down to we call it crew cuts.

I remember I was going around the colleges, the wards, cutting hair and shaving, and it came on a special news bulletin on the TV that Dr. Martin Luther King got shot in Memphis. People was sad out there; they was very very upset that he got shot; they was crying, the patients was crying. I was crying too, 'cause he was trying to help people — poor people, black and white — out: to be equal. He fought for civil rights. They didn't let a colored lady sit up front and I guess that's how it came about.

And I moved from the barbershop over to the storeroom; we used to get supplies ready to go on colleges — chewing tobacco, smokin' tobacter, shoes. Trucks would come in with big boxes of cereals, frozen vegetables. and we would shoot them down into the kitchen, would put them in the freezer, and the dry stuff, like sugar, we would store them in the storage area.

I had bosses there; they was 'tendants. I liked to work with anybody that worked; I didn't have a special choice who I wanted to work with.

I was answering the phones and taking messages; picking up little kids from the hospital and bringing them to school. I assisted the gym teacher in the summertime, taking kids to summer school and day camp and activities. They had a printing press, a greenhouse; I didn't used to work there, but on the farm. They had a farm. Shorty McVeigh took us down there. We used to pick string beans, red beets, carrots, cabbage, sweet potatoes, corn on the cob, potatoes, broccoli, asparagus, greens, and put 'em in the basket. We used to bring baskets full of tomatoes to the kitchen. A farmer guy used to drive the tractor. They had nine, ten acres. They used to grow their own vegetables. And they used to have ponies — just to pet them. I used to work in the patients' dining room; I used to run the dishwasher and clean things off the tables. After people would leave the dining room, we would collect the dishes and spoons and silverwares, and put them in that dish room, and we would wash the dishes.

I was doing other things up there. I used to work in the laundry. We get to go on the truck around the colleges and pick up the dirty soiled linen and take 'em to the laundry. And then I used to work the back of the washing machine, where they washed dirty linen — the sheets and towels and night pajamas — and put them in the big washing machines. We used to put things in the dryer and take them out and sort them and put them in a hamper bag, and take the sheets and put them there on the other side, so they can be run through the big machines, starched, and then folded up. That give me some things to do; keep me busy; to get me ready for being on the rehabilitation.

And then from the laundry they transferred me to the staff cafeteria. They had a woman there that takes care of job placement. She figured where I was going to work. That was just getting me ready to go out on the outside, preparing you for the outside. She transferred me into the staff cafeteria. I used to run the dishwasher over there. That felt good, because I was getting good food in there. The patients would get horrible food: had eyes in the potatoes, half cooked, steamed. And attendants would get very good food than the patients. In the attendants' cafeteria their food would get fried — well cooked; their food was cooked thoroughly.

We would eat first and then we would open up twenty-five after eleven and go through until two. And that's how I used to learn how to do all this getting the salad and making food. I used to get up at five o'clock in the morning to get ready to go to work. I would start to work in the in the attendants' cafeteria around about quarter of seven. And I had to have the cafeteria clean by 'leven o'clock to get ready for lunch. And that was a big 'sponsibility. We used to put all the chairs up on the tables so we can mop the floor and buff the floor; then we would cover all the tables with tablecloths.

I would have to be at work at a certain time and work the whole day through til at night. And when I get finish, I used to walk around on the grounds, just walk around, up and down, back and forth, where the superintendent lived. Up the hill, halfway up the girls' county [colony — K.W.], and down the hill, down the boys' side. We used to just walk up and down the road, back and forth up and down there.

I even worked as a messenger at Pennhurst, taking messages back and forth. I liked running errands the best; it was really fun to do that.

I got to know the switchboard operator; I used to take the time sheets down to the administration building — the teachers' payroll. That was where the superintendent's office is. And this is where they did the hearing tests and psychological evaleration. Nobody lived there. All the offices would be closed Saturdays and Sundays. I learned by looking at the letters; they had the letters outside the building: they would tell me that, "Hey, this is the A Building." That's where all different envelopes would go: the records, once-a-month report about the school, and the census, annual report. So I used to take the messenger's envelopes to different places. And answer phones.

We never got — nobody I know of — never got paid, not actually paid money. We got tokens that we would go to the canteen and buy things with the token. Unless you went to the canteen for them or store to get a cup of coffee or doughnuts or whatever — they would write a piece of paper what they want; we would bring it back to the staff; they would give us a dime or a nickel or a quarter. Never got paid. Nobody got paid. They would work, work, work, work — never see the check up there. Nothing.

I used to work in the P building. When the visitors used to come, we would wait for them to write out a slip and they would give me a slip to take to the wards and get their sons and dress them. You would have to dress them and bring them back to their family. They had like nightgowns on — the low ones

— and they had like underwears. We would get them and take them to another ward to get their regular clothes on. I would take the note there and another staff would give them clothes. And we used to get tips. The visitors would give a tip; you could earn some money. That would be like your allowance and you save it up, get a radio or TV or something, if you want it.

When my father retired off his work, I used to get part of his disability money; they would send me a check every month; the Social Security would send it, 'cause I was eligible for part of his Social Security. I was the only person in the family could get it. My mother told me that was because I was the only retarded person in the family that could get it — disability. He took a heart attack on the job and he couldn't work any more. The doctor told him he couldn't do that heavy work, getting underneath the cars, and breathing that stuff in. I would get a check. They stopped giving tokens and gave me real cash money. They would type my name on the paper and we would get paid every Thursday evening. Not from the job, from SSI; I would request how much I want.

They moved me around. I would work in the mornings: all day in the morning, all day in the evening. There was different jobs. I was too old enough to go to school at that time; I graduated, in other words; and I got older. They would try me on different jobs; get me ready for the outside. Some people had one job and they stayed with their job, I guess, til after they left. They was just trying to get me prepared for the outside. They switched me around to see what type of job I could be suited for. I did well.

Once I walked off the job — I was so depressed. Oh, I had enough of Pennhurst! Oh, yes. I just walked up and down the corridor on the hospital ward. I had cut myself and they had to suture me. I was just scared, just frightened. That's true. I would be frightened, very very frightened — what next I would do, what next would they do; what next, what next. I been on every ward that they trained me on; I been on everything — I did from bathing, washing dishers — dishwasher — working in the barbershop, working in the laundry; and I did mostly all the things that they taught me, so there was no need to train me again. I walked off the job because I was just depressed.

• • •

They moved me down to Penn Hall 1 and I lived down there for nine months. That's more like getting ready to go on the outside, to live in the community. They teach you how to respect other people. And they told me how to save money and they gave me a town pass. There was no attendants. We was doing it all ourselves, taking care of the house and making sure the house is kept clean. There was attendants come over, used to take a rag and see any dust or any dirt on the dresser on the windowsill. Every time we would get a star for it, for excellent; and if it was dirty, we would get a red star, meaning it wasn't too cool. We had to make sure our clothes was washed. We used to get our food from the dining room; we would put an order in, send a list over to the dining room and we would pick up the food from the dining room.

It was very nice. Nice attendants. We got some hobbies; we made some stuff, turkeys and vases, out of clay and you put 'em in a kiln and we paint 'em and spray 'em. And we'd make ashtrays out of records, melt them like that.

And then I was moved to Rehab 1 up there; it used to be a white house. And they used to train us to cook and make our own beds and go out to work every day. It was teaching you how to be more independent. And it was very nice being on independent without somebody looking over you.

And I got myself better and better and better. Getting better means getting things more sharper like — I got a sense of what's going on. It took me a long while to think why I was sent there, why I was put there at Pennhurst. I gave my mother so much problem. It took me a long time to understand it. And it dawned on me as to why I'm put there in the first place at Pennhurst: they had no where else to put me, so I had to go there. It taught me about my life.

I thought that the doors would be open one day, back open for me to go home again; it might be a day, as I got older, that you might be get out.

We used to get town passes and go into Pottstown, shopping or watching the movies. I would eat up in Pottstown. There was a diner I used to love so much up there; people used to know us from just going back and just eating. Would be two of us going together.

I had a girl friend, Shirley R. I met her in the school building. She was coming to school and she would stop me for different things. She would stop me in the schoolyard and she would ax me do I have any money. And I said, "No, not this time." And she said, "When you gonna get some money?" I said, "I don't know." So I said, "When I meet you again I'll have some money."

And she would ax me: "You want to be my boyfriend?" I said, "Boyfriend! Naa, c'mon — you're putting me on." And then I just said, "Okay."

And then we dated; we went places, Pottstown, and stuff like that. I would walk her back and forth to the girls' county. We'd kiss. I'd be kissing her and going around with her.

She used to work in the 'tendants' cafeteria along with me. And I just used to help her out. I used to give her a Christmas present and wrap it up and give it to her. She give me a Christmas present; it was a shirt and gloves. I gave her a radio. And things like that.

And we talked in the school hallway. She would use me, try to get money out of me. She'd ax me, "Do you have any money?" "I don't got no money this time — maybe next time." She would just keep coming to me about money. And every time I'd bump into her — "Roland, you have any money? I need to buy something." "Well, I don't have any money this time." And she says, "Oh, please — you got money." And she kept forcing it out of me. So I gave her ten dollars. Every time I would get paid, I would give her some little bit of money to help her.

And she would be bad in school; she would sit in the principal's office. It was just something. Yeah, she liked me. Me and her used to go skating together, up Pottstown. Well, the girls'd go first and then the boys would go last; we'd meet together up there.

We used to dance together. They had the canteen up there. I used to buy candy and hot dogs and sometimes french fries and hamburgers. I would meet her at the canteen down on the boys' side.

Me and her got along very good, but it was tough for both of us. She would make you laugh, she would; she would make funny jokes. I had nice hair; my hair wasn't like this, my back hair wasn't like that; I had really bushy hair like Michael Jackson when they was small — bushy hair, long hair — I left my hair grow. And she would laugh: "Why don't you just get a haircut? Get a haircut!" And everybody would laugh at me. "Oh, look at this; look at this guy; look at this young boy — he looks like Alfalfa with his hair all crooked up." I think she meant Buckwheat. And she would tease me and her friends would tease me, "Look at that boy." I just got a joke out it. "What are you teasing me for? People's wearing their hair this way." Bush. My hair would just grow out and it was just like bush. My mother come up and see me and she said, "Next time I come up here you better get that hair off." The attendants didn't care — it was your hair. But sooner or later I hadda got it cut: the barber said, "I couldn't get through all this hair on you with the clippers." I had a comb; I had a part in it and waves.

And we used to be kissing in the hallway in the school. She was a tough one; she was a cookie. I liked the girl. She liked me. I don't know if she just liked me for my money, or what. But I used to talk to her a lot for a year, two years. She would meet these other boys — I think she was using me, to get money out of me. You know how girls are. Oh, I was about seventeen; she was about eighteen. She'd come into school after I had class; she would meet me in the upstairs hallway. And then the other boys would get jealous. They'd say, "Why was you laughing? Why are you going with him for? He doesn't look right for you! To me, he doesn't look right you going with him. You ought to go with me." I didn't want to get into that, so she stopped seeing me and I stopped seeing her. She would write letters to me. And I would — 'cause I couldn't write — I would get somebody to read the letters for me. She says, "I love you and I want you to be my boyfriend." La-la-la … "When we get out, if we both get out, we can meet each other," 'cause she lived in Philadelphia. We used to talk about good things — how we're going to get out: "If you get out before I do, would you give me a call? And if I get out before you, I'll give you a call. And write to me."

Right now, to the day, I don't know where she is. Because I didn't have her address. She was sent there under a court case as a child, sixteen years old she was. She had other sisters; they couldn't get along together. That was about all that she told me. She left first and then I left second. I think she went back to her mother at home. We said that we would call each other, but we never kept up with it. I didn't see her after that. I did say that I would try to stay in contact with her, but it was very hard, to stay contact with her. She gave me her address and I lost it in the shuffle, because when I left Pennhurst my mother and father came and got me and I lost the book.

In order to get your town pass it had to be two people. Two people would go together. My name came up and they just gave it to me. I had a friend with me that showed me how to do that. He was walking with me and I was following. We would walk outside and down the road and wait there and the bus would come. You would show your town pass. The bus driver would know us, because people from Pennhurst would go up there every Saturday.

I did run away from Pennhurst couple times. I don't think it was called runaway; I was just going to the store — a bunch of us used to sneak off the grounds. I remember I snuck away on the railroad track to Royersford; it was real cold — real low to freezing mark. We walked down to Spring City — me and some other friend of mine — bought ice cream, and snuck back before eleven o'clock, before the other shift came on.

I was lonely at Pennhurst, all the time. I was always wanting someone to come and see me to talk to. I was very, very, very, very lonely. I wonder why I went to Pennhurst, but things came to me while I went to Pennhurst. I never understand it until I was around eighteen. I understand it, when I was at Pennhurst. That's why: because I did some things that I should not have done. It make me sorrowful and grief. It helped me in some areas but it didn't help me in other areas.

Pennhurst didn't meant nothing to me. Pennhurst was me with sorrows and grief. I didn't like it at all.

BOARDING HOMES

The teacher helped me to write a letter to my mother. I axed my mother, "This place is horrible" and "What could you do to get me out of here, out of Pennhurst? Would you please give this a little 'sideration in trying to re-samine me and look at me and see the change and the difference in me?" And then she wrote back to me and someone read the letter to me and said that, "Yes, your mother said she's going to look into that and she's going to write to Dr. Potkonski and see what's going on with you." And at the time that she wrote to Dr. Potkonski, it went to Mr. Claypoole. He was a also social worker. So he went and visit my mother and told my mother, "Why don't you look at this and examine him and bring him home as a trial base and see how it goes. After six months, if he has no changes, then we consider that he's not ready for being in the community." So she told the high official, Mr. Claypoole, she said that she think that she was ready to be with me at home.

It was fun when I first came home. The first time I met everybody, they was talking to me and it was just like, "Hey, I'm not in this big institution anymore. This crazy old institution." I talked a little bit about Pennhurst and I said that I didn't want to go back there no more. The more they talked to me and the more my mother heard me talk, she said she was amazed how they kind of worked with you. But I told her, "That's not so; I just picked that up as I went along" ... talking like "Yes, ma'am," "No, ma'am," "No, thank you." I still had a little mischievin'

61

mischief in me. But I still was frightened of my mother, because maybe she was going to do the same thing back. Then well I guess that she said, "Well, yes, I think we can have him home for good." I was so tickled to death that she said this.

And then Mr. Claypoole came out and told my mother, "He's only home for a trial period. And if he does anything wrong, just give us a call, and you can bring him right back." After that I didn't go back in. That's when Mom was very, very proud. "That was a big change in you, boy. You're not stealing nothing."

When my mother was working I used to be at home by myself. And I would walk over to my sister's house. I had to walk down over a bridge and walk near a park and then from there I went over to my oldest sister's, Alvera's, house, and I'd spend some time over there with her. Her daughter would play the piano, 'cause she was an organist and a piano player. She plays music good. In the Johnson family we all have music ability. Sissy — Alvera — was the choir director at Christian Union.

When I came out of Pennhurst I would go over and stay and visit my sister Bertha May. And I would go over Bootsie's house, Eleanor. I did a lot of walking. I would walk over there and talk to her for a while; ax her about Pinkie and Candy and Terry; she's got a lot of children; can't name 'em all. And every time they'd see me, I would give them like fifty cents; they would love when I come over.

A little they did have to watch me, but not as much. I don't know why that was; I don't know what was different, being there. I think Alvera knew me and she kept her eyes on me.

I didn't have to learn how to use SEPTA [Southeastern Pennsylvania Transit Authority — K.W.]. I knew it all the time, how to use SEPTA. At any time I could go down to Broad and

Spring Garden Street and go on the second floor and see my counselor. I knew the C bus; I knew everything. Nobody had to show me; I just knew it.

• • •

I made up my mind that I had to leave because I wasn't getting along at home very well. I wanted to move from my mother because I was getting on her nerves. I wanted to be on my own, so I tried to live with another family, but that did not go well at all.

The first boarding home I went to was Mrs. W. My mother didn't send me; I went. I was living with Mrs. Katherine W. in 1972. The house was nice. She had some of Pennhurst people; we slept in a room together, three people, and she slept upstairs. It was no better than Pennhurst. I didn't like it there. I didn't like the food; she put different things in food that I didn't like for my taste. She made me eat it.

And Mrs. W. take all your money; when the social security checks come, she took it all. I didn't like it there at all. She told me if I didn't get out of the bed, she would get her son to turn the mattress over and throw me out of bed. I put in a long day at work and I must have slept a long time on Saturday. I was working at PARC Workshop. Before I went to PARC [Philadelphia Association for Retarded Citizens — K.W.] my cousin recommended me to Minuteman's Car Wash in North Philly, Broad and Lehigh. Washing cars — drying cars off and washing cars. They would drop tips in the box when the car came out. These people was like ... they drink a lot; I didn't make too many friends. At PARC I was working on the machine, packing sponges. Mrs. W. told me I had to do Saturday's chores around the house. So I slept. Probably she didn't like that. 'Cause the others that lived there with her, they're doing their chores, and I didn't do my chores. I just didn't care too much about it. She made her son turn the mattress out of bed to get me out. She was not a nice person at all. She was mean. She hit me. The social worker said that I had to move back to my mother because Mrs. W. didn't want me living there any more with her. I had to go back to my mother. And then that's where I stayed.

And then I was hollering at my mother. A person across the street on Cleveland Street, a boy, thought that I was making motions with him — making motions to come here or something like that. But that wasn't true, that I was making motions at him. I hollered at my mother and she was very ill and she couldn't take it and so she called somebody. She called somebody and told them that, "I can't handle my son no more. Would you find a place for him?" And the case manager told my mother there was a person who takes care of people that Roland might like, that's in his age level. So I had to pack up all my clothes and move out of the house. I got moved from my mother to Mrs. P.'s boarding home.

And I liked it there; she fed us good. But I had to do all the cleaning. It was elderly people that she was taking care of. And I was about the youngest person there. And this guy died in the next room. He had been sick and he just expired. She told me to pick him up from the rolling chair and put him in the bed. I thought he was asleep. She didn't even tell me that he was dead. She made me pick up a dead body that I wasn't supposed to pick up. I give him a bath and everything so the family could come and see him. See, he was cripple, so he couldn't get a bath. We had to give everybody a bath in a bathtub. I put him in the bathtub, washed him, bathed him, and took him out and rolled the sheets down and put him in the bed. I was scared. I guess he died in the afternoon. She didn't tell me that person was deceased. She kept a clean house; it was a nice place, but that other part I didn't like. So I axed to be removed.

And then I went from there, from that boarding house, to Mrs. T., Marion T. The cops had to come and drag me out of her house, 'cause me and Timothy got in a difficult argument. Timothy used to be a patient at Woodhaven. He said I ripped his pants, his new suit. And I didn't do it. And I got very upset. And the police threw me against the wall and threw me in the truck, the paddy wagon, and it hurt my head and I didn't like that at all. So they took me to the North Central crisis center. They took X-rays, but there was no broken.

Well, she told me she didn't want me back. So I knocked her table over, trying to grab at her. Her son was a police, but he called another police to take me to the crisis center at Temple.

And then I went to Mr. B.'s boarding home, from Mrs. T. And I stayed there for a while and then I moved out for a while. It was older, more older people than I. Mr. B. didn't live there; he would collect the rent, but he didn't live there. A next-door neighbor was taking care of the house. Things was pretty good there, but I axed to move out of there and then I went to North Central and ax 'em can I find a better place. I axes. This is my life story.

I was in lots of boarding homes. I went from one boarding home to another. I was living at Fernderry, West Lehigh Avenue, Mrs. M. I bought a brand-new ten-speed bicycle at one of the bicycle stores in Germantown. And three weeks after I got the bike I had an accident. My friend I met in Fernderry, Charley Marshall, he said, "Let's go riding." So I went riding with him and I turned the corner and here comes the speeding cars. I was riding on Broad Street, Broad and Airy, and no sooner or later all I knew I was hit by something — by a car. It threw me up in the air; bicycle went too. I was in the hospital; had my leg up in traction, one leg, the left. My mother came and seen me and she said, "How did you do that?" So I told her that I got hit and run. "Didn't I tell you not to ride bicycles?" my mother said. "Did you get the person's ... Did anybody see it?" I guess nobody seen it; there was nothing to tell the police, 'cause you couldn't say who it was. I couldn't put charges.

I went back to Fernderry; it was just another place, a YWCA and the Y moved out and they turned it into a boarding home.

I left out one more person — Mrs. Amy T. I lived at that boarding home. I wasn't treated well there either. I had to do the same thing that I was doing at somebody else's house. So my life was just mixed up — running from place to place. All these places.

All the boarding homes take your money and they only give you about five dollars out of it.

Later on PARC got me a job. 'Cause I went through all the necessary steps, so they couldn't keep me there putting spoons in plastic bags and counting screws and nuts and bolts.

They got me a job working at Mr. Lerner's — Lerner Luncheonette — Lou Lerner's. I was chef's helper: repairing onions, taking things off the onions; preparing potatoes, and scraping carrots and chopping carrots and putting meats away when it come and taking orders out to different people at lunch time. And I would earn tips. Yeah it was good pay. Until someone stopped me when I was coming home from work. They almost took my check; they tried to grab me walking down the street. And they say, "Hey, you! Turn over your money! You got any money on you?" I said no. "Just check your pocket!" So they tried to get it, but they couldn't — I ran.

I found a job up in Stenton Avenue, Washington Lane; I worked there for three years. I was a dishwasher, helping make food and salads and cut up onions and stuff. I used to come in in the morning, eight o'clock, and work til closing time, in the summertime and in the winter — about nine, nine-thirty. The boss' name was Mr. Foster; the other fellow that had it didn't want it no more, so he bought it from the other boss. This was a diner restaurant. Everybody was doing their job like; only time you could talk together was having a lunch break. And that's about it. 'Cause the place was always kept busy. Yeah, that was a pretty large check. Mrs. P. would just take what I would get from SSI. I put this work check in the bank. I did it all by myself. I was going to buy things with that money — Christmas gifts for my family, all my sisters and brothers and nephews and nieces, my mother and father. It was very exciting.

Oh, I had lots of jobs.

From there I went to the Barclay Hotel, Rittenhouse Square. I was housekeeping: vacuum cleaning the rugs and shampooing; mopping the floors; washing the mirrors; and the trash. It was pretty big; lots of floors to do. They had good benefits: like insurance benefits — if you get sick they would automatically pay for your health benefit and the insurance would send you a check for yourself. I got sick; I couldn't keep that job too long; I had seizures.

I fell in their laundry room. I was coming downstairs to put my bucket and stuff away — I left at four thirty — and no sooner later my hands was starting to shake and my body was shaking and I had a seizure. I felled on the floor and had a seizure. My supervisor, Mrs. S., called my mother and she couldn't know what to do. They all got scared; they got very panicked on the

… I never had a seizure before. And I understand that the police had to come and handcuff me. I was throwing things around and shaking and hurting people and they had to hold me down on the job. This was in the summertime. And they called my mother and she didn't know what to do, so they rushed me to Graduate Hospital. They said they was seizures. They was giving me medicine — Dilantin and phenobarbs and other kind of medicines. They did the brain scan; they would put all these 'lectrical wires on me. Nothing showed up on the electricals. They put me on lots of different medicines; they tried different medicines. I would take two medicines a day for seizures. And I think that about every hospital I been in, they tell me they was fake seizures. They call it "panic attacks." And they was not fake seizures. Dr. Gross, my doctor now, took me off it. He calls them "body seizures," "pseudo-seizures." They're not actually seizures from the brain — you be thinking about something and then it connects some of them wires in the brain. People have it in war, when they come out of it. When you get upset or depressed — it has nothing to do with the brain itself; it has nothing to do with that. Shellshock — Dr. Nettleton says that a lot. [Dr. Carol Cobb Nettleton, Roland's counselor — K.W.] When people was in the service they get shellshock; they get very panic and they have pseudo-seizures — but they are seizures.

So I stayed in there, in Graduate Hospital; that's how come I knew that my father passed away. My brother came up and told me, William — he came and visit me.

He had been sick with a heart attack. He died at home in my mama's arms. He got up to go to the bathroom; it was 'round five o'clock in the morning, he died.

They gave me off on my job to go to the funeral. Oh, it was a big funeral, my father's funeral. He knew a lot of people around the neighborhood on Elsworth Street and people from North Philly on North Cleveland Street. He had a funeral in a funeral home, 'cause he didn't have no church home; he didn't go to church like my mother.

He went to church one night — I understand that he was standing up in the church and one of his friends had pulled him by his suit tail and said, "Sit down." He was standing up for a long while. I guess he was testifying or something.

But that night he knew when he was ready; he told my mother that he was ready to go. He knew that he was going to die; he wasn't afraid.

He died of a heart attack. That's what he retired for. He did a little bit of work, 'cause he never keep still. My mother would say, "Roy, you know you can't go out there and work under them cars. Because you're gonna have another heart attack." And he says, "I have to keep busy; I have to keep busy." He would come home and sit on the chair — like I got in my living room — he would just be singing to himself, be singing some hymns; and he would just be his ordinary self. He was just happy — smile on his face — always happy.

I was in a lot of several hospitals; I was in and out of the hospitals — couple times in Graduate Hospital, couple times in Temple Hospital, couple times in Women's Medical College of Pennsylvania, and Hahnemann Hospital. I had a kidney stone. I had a keloid infection. They had to shave part of the skin off at Women's Medical; Dr. James C. performed the operation. I was not with my mother at that time; I was on Lehigh Avenue. I was combing my hair and all the hair came out and left sores on my scalp. I was scratching — I got it from barber clippers. I never had sores in my head up until I went to the barber shop; I had nice hair. The doctor said it was just a ringworm infection; I went to a skin doctor and he said it was an infection that they couldn't cure; they put me on all kinds of medicine; it just didn't help. It started in the back and worked itself up into my scalp and inside the skin. And I had gotten a very high fever from it and they put me in the hospital and they did the surgery.

That's when I got my life back together. I was confused in a lot of areas, running from one boarding home to another boarding home to another boarding home to another boarding home. I got myself straightened out through North Central; they put me in a CLA [Community Living Arrangement — K.W.] and Mrs. Willie May Samuels thought that I should be in a day program since I didn't work then. It was a partial hospital day program, a mental health program, like a psychiatric day program to get people to get theirself better and go back out in the community. Well, it helped me to better myself.

The patients they ran it themselves; they set up the program. It was a day program that you had to go every day start from 8:30 to 3:30; you could not sit at home. It was right across on Lehigh Avenue; there was a restaurant downstairs. At the end of the morning meetings we had broke up with small groups and we'd go from ten o'clock to quarter to twelve and we would talk about our problems, emotional problems, or whatever problems that you had on your mind. We would all come back together and eat lunch together. It would be ten people in different groups. The patients would run the morning meetings; they would have questions of whatever they had on their minds. And we would talk out our problems.

I was shy within myself. I was scared when all these people come around. I remember that, being shy. I just forced myself. I talked in the groups and they listened.

Some people would get up and talk about their life story, how they got into the program and how they got in trouble. These were people that had been on drugs, people had emotional problems, alcoholic problems, problems with the family. These are people that could not deal with their life. And that kind of helped me; that kind of put things back to the place.

Agencies was moving around a lot; North Central phrased out and Comprehensive took to over for a while. That's when I heard about Speaking for Ourselves. It was when my life started to change around.

Roland at Speaking For Ourselves Planning Retreat at Fellowship Farm

SPEAKING FOR OURSELVES

The organization already started when I first heard about Speaking For Ourselves. I was working at Germantown and Lycoming workshop. I was a janitor at that time, outside the workshop. It was a man named Russell Donohue; he had said that there was a conference going on at Valley Forge at the Holiday Inn. He probably got it from a literature that they had. He was telling everybody, so he axed everybody who wanted to go to raise their hands and I raised my hand that I wanted to go. So we made a list and went to the conference on their big van.

The conference was a whole bunch of people that I didn't know. And I heard all these people talking about their life and I remember Domenic Rossi standing up there saying, "We need to get things together; we need people's life changed. It's time to do and not talk about it — let's do it." And Luann Carter was running the conference; she was the founder of Speaking For Ourselves. They started out real small. They had a small little group — it was just Mark [Mark Friedman has been advisor to the board of Speaking For Ourselves since its inception. — K.W.] and some other people — and it grew and grew — started in Montgomery County, then Bucks, Delaware, and Philadelphia, and Chester.

That very first conference I was wearing jeans. I was working and I had these dirty old jeans on; they wasn't dirty, but they had spots; I was scrubbing the floor and I was stripping the wax off the floor, the old wax, and putting down fresh wax. I had my work shoes on. And Mark says, "Who's that guy back there?

75

Who's that guy back there, standing up?" I just stood up in the back and said, "We have to make some changes!" in front of a whole lot of people. I was always talking about it, 'bout getting things changed, making things more better for the clients. Wasn't for me. Was for all the people that have disabilities. I was just thinking about it. And nobody told me to say. I just was thinking about it — the system needs to be changed. So I just stood up in the back and said, "It should be changed. We're tired of the old system. We're tired of the system that we have now. We need to make things change, to make things happen." And that's when I first met Mark Friedman.

I went to the night school; I was in a CLA program. They had mental retardation night, Wednesday night school at Girl's High: how to read, how to write, say your letters, ABC's, and stuff like that. And Nancy Nowell [advisor to the Philadelphia Chapter — K.W.] came to Girl's High. Nancy explained that Speaking For Ourselves was for people with disabilities — to get their rights, be heard, and speak up with whatever is on their mind. Well, they couldn't find a room to hold their meetings, so they had it at Girls' High, Broad and Olney, downstairs in the classroom, a kitchen like. So I went down.

It was a lot of people; it was very lot of people. I don't know how many that came. And Eleanor Elkins, [an internationally recognized parent advocate — K.W.] she was there. And Nancy Nowell. I thought for a while that they was running the organization, because Eleanor Elkins has a son that's retarded and I think that she wanted more things better for her son and better for the organization. But I don't think that they was running it; they would want the members to run the organization.

I went for a while. And then I stopped going for a while.

And then they switched it over to Osteopathic Hospital out on City Line Avenue.

And it struck me that these people was saying things for themselves, speaking up for themselves. I knew that they was going to nominate me as president — I thought of that myself — because I was the person that was on the ball, had the skills, had the know-how.

And the group voted me as the president of the chapter.

Domenic was the president of the Board of Directors for the whole organization. I would talk to him on the phone. We would talk about how would I get my chapter more involved, to make the things happen in the chapter. We talked over hours on the phone; he helped me, I helped him. So that's how I got involved in Speaking for Ourselves.

We had to talk to people at Osteopathic — could we use their space. Nancy and Mark and me went. We didn't have to ax them for chairs. They said, "You can use whatever's in there. You take the chairs and use them." We put the chairs back like they had them after we left. It was the president's job to appoint somebody to do that; sometimes I would help to do it. It was very pleasant to have us come there. Sometime twenty or thirty people would show.

My job was to make sure cards, notices about the next meeting, got out. Me and Nancy wrote out letters to get people to come. Mark had a computer; we could get the names off the computer, but we had got some more, new people. We had to go out and make ourselves known, that there is an organization that exists, that there is a Speaking For Ourselves. We send members to go out and speak to the county office and the state officials to talk about whatever was on their mind to talk about. And that's how I got to go to these places.

Speaking For Ourselves helped me to be more talkable, more open, and more understanding. At the time I was afraid of people. I was scared of people. I didn't like to share things with people and I didn't think that they would listen to me, whatever I said. I thought that the organization was a very good organization. Speaking For Ourselves was like a friendly organization — more homelike; it was an organization to come to to express yourself. Speaking For Ourselves had open my eyes to be a better person and try to help other people. There is joy for something for everybody to do, that everybody want to do — always something involved, that I'm involved with something, constantly something to do, like going to meetings, setting up meetings, going out and talking to people. I like to give more into people, more express to people that Speaking For Ourself is very good and people need to be involved. I just try to help people and give back into the community. It just came naturally.

It wasn't hard for me. They listened pretty good. I knew how to kept order 'cause I'm always pleasant. I was pleasant with them and I said that, "If you want Speaking For Ourselves, you have to do the things that members do: this is Speaking For Ourselves and you have to talk up." And so the people was quiet. I got them talking, got them to talk for themselves, to speak for themselves. I made people get a chance to talk and say whatever they got on their mind. I said, "Would you like to talk — whatever is on your mind: what happened in your group homes or what happened in your CLA programs. You're here; what you say here stays here — it'll never go out." That was our policy.

The chapter meetings are just very informal. They talked about jobs: they wanted jobs; they didn't want be in workshops, they wanted to get out on their own, 'cause they don't make too much in workshops. They talked about transportation; transportation was the big issue. Every time we have our chapter meeting, it was "How will we get to our chapter — we don't have transportation." We had a young girl come in from SEPTA Paratransit and talk about how can we make Paratransit better for people with disability; how could we make transportation better for them. And we talked on and on about different things. They would talk about what things going on in their life where they live. It would go on about an hour or so and then we shift it onto another topic. We would talk about, "I wasn't getting along in my CLA, because I was being abused by the system" — problem solving.

The staff would find out and the director would find out, some kind of way — you can't help it. "Well, you went and told them people that you did not like it here, so you don't go to that meeting." That's what would happen. So we would be losing our attendance.

It was my job to make sure that everybody get a chance. The thing about it was, they looked up to me, that "There's a man is giving me a chance to talk." They looked up at me. I don't know what they looked up at me for, but they looked up: "There he is." So I said, "Come on, talk. Don't be shy. Talk. That's why we're here for. Talk. Anything that you got on your mind, talk. Talk about it. Whatever you talk about in here, stays here; it will never go out nowhere else." And they talk about problems that they have every day, that they have on their minds.

Some of them talk about they didn't like their home, their living situation; they was not being treated well; the staff overspent their money, took their money. They talked about, "My staff hurt me." I know a guy came to our chapter and he talked almost over an hour, talked about a specific staff person that he didn't like. "I want that staff person moved out. I don't like that staff." It was very hard putting the pieces together. Very hard.

Well, I told him, "If it happens again, you bring it back to the chapter, and we'll ... we'll fix it for you. We'll get somebody to work on it." And he brought it back and we moved.

I remember telling one of our members, "You know by not joining Speaking For Ourselves, you would not better as you was gotten better today? When you first came to Speaking For Ourselves you was quiet, in your little shell. But when you got used to Speaking For Ourselves, you really talking now; you really expressing yourself; you really coming out of your shell."

And they really did! And that's where it showed me, helped me to understand a lot of things about this organization. They had some power behind the organization.

• • •

Nancy axed me, "You might want to come out and look at the Board of Directors." So I came, one Thursday. That's when they had their board meetings, once a month. These was held at Plymouth Meeting Mall. I was still a chapter president. I went to the Board of Directors meetings before I came to be president. And then when that chapter president was ended, then I went to the board. And that's when I guess I got elected as president at the board. I was appointed by the Board of Directors as the President of the Board of the Directors of Speaking For Ourselves.

Domenic was the board president before I got to be president. We talked together. Yeah, I went to him; we had several meetings about what should I do. I didn't know nothing about the role of being a president. So Domenic taught me about being a president. The board had a lot of things to do: keep the minutes and keeping people on time. He said to keep order and make sure the records are straight before they audit it and how to do Mark's evaluation once a year. He said, "You got to work with Mark; he's a hard man to work with; you got to hang in there with him; you got to keep him on target on everything." So I took his advice; I kept Mark on the ball. "Come on, Mark, on the ball. Stay off the phone." Domenic meant that Mark just talks a lot and can't concentrate well on a lot of things. He gave me some strong advice. We got Domenic a job as the treasurer, taking care of the books, writing out the checks and stuff.

The board meeting went from six-thirty to nine o'clock. Usual, we would be out of there by nine. But it was just talking about business, what to do. When the first time that I was president I said, "Gee, I don't know if I have the skills to do that."

We was closed out for the summer and when we started back up in September we only had a few people come to the board and I said to Mark, "Where's all the members? Where are the Board of Directors? Where's everybody at? I'm kind of scared. Did I do something last year that made it something different this September? Are they scared because I'm a black person? Maybe they ain't showing because I'm a black colored person. Maybe that's why they ain't all showing, because I'm black."

He said, "Oh, that's not it. That's not it at all."

"I don't see them, I don't. I'm the president and I'm kinda scared. I don't know."

He said, "Maybe they had something to do; maybe that's why they didn't show."

"Maybe ... Maybe so."

And I was so nervous, shaking in my boots. That here am I — I'm in this board meeting, all by myself, and nobody shows up. It was only me and Mark and Nancy and Domenic.

It took me a while to get over that. Mark got me to pay attention of the presidency, to talk to people more and stop being shy. I got over it; I didn't think of that for long. Like I said, I had courage enough to do all this. I said, "We just do this, Mark." And it was faith, my faith: This is going to happen. Sooner or later, this is going to happen. No doubts. It's going to happen.

Very hard to express — to see a colored person being something of a leader of a organization like Speaking for Ourselves. Was the first time for a colored person, being a colored president of a board, of taking in charge of something that he never had tooken charge. And this is something that I looked forward to being someday — the first black colored person that has a handicap disability would help to steer people in the right direction.

We had to call everybody up and tell 'em that it was very serious; that you had to come; there's some things that we have to talk about. I told 'em, "Don't do that again, 'cause this is very important meeting that we have to talk about and we have to get things organized on the board level."

I helped changed things around.

People had been getting up going to the bathroom interrupting the Board of Directors while the meetings was going on. And I said that we could not do this because I can't function while people are going to the bathroom — that's not how a board of directors should operate, people getting up and going to the bathroom and running around, giggling, and stuff like that.

I had been to other kinds of meetings in the partial hospitalization day program. It taught me a lot — how to conduct a meeting, how to select officers, how to focus on different things. And people could not jump up and go to the bathroom, getting up and just being outside in the hall — that does not work that way. I learned that then.

I talked with Mark about that, that we had to do some changes, or else when people come, they'll say, "Hmph. I don't know about this. I don't know about this board. That don't seem like a board meeting to me, with a lot of people running around up and down." I had told Mark that he couldn't get up and go to the bathroom because people see that and they'll follow him, because that's not being a good example for them. Suppose somebody comes in, somebody from the State, and everybody goes to the bathroom; that wouldn't be fair. Or the President of the United States — you invited the President — that wouldn't be nice, running out. So you have to maintain some kind of order in your board of directors meeting.

It was a struggle to make the board understand this. We had to get this in place before my term ran out; if we didn't, it would be the same thing happening as we didn't do this, put this into action. It was very serious. I was very serious about putting this thing into action, getting the board on the right track: stop running to the bathroom and sit and listen. It took two months to get my act together.

I went home and think, then I call up Mark and I said, "Well, you know, Mark, sometimes I'm thinking I'm too bossy. Maybe people won't believe me all the time; maybe they don't know what I'm saying."

Oh, it was big headache to make this work; it wouldn't work it. Something was gonna fold or they would elected another president.

But we did it. We did it together.

I was the type of person that's strict, very strict — but pleasant — to make it run more smoothly. Whatever I said, went. Well, maybe everybody didn't agree with what I said, but some of it slowed down. I taught them what I taught them, what I learned.

And they looked up to me as a leader. So that's how things changed.

After two years I got them to settle down. I told them that you have to stay focused on what you're doing and you have to listen to the president. The president's in charge and you have to listen to what's on the agenda. To make a good board leader you have to make people listen and stay focused on what you're talking about. I said, "We're not going to get up and down and run around. We're going to concentrate on the things that it's on the agenda."

Whoever came, that person would think, "Well, hmm. I never seen any board meeting 'ducted that nice. They conducted themselves very nice; it was not emotional." That would help them to understand, that would teach them, it would say to them, "Well, there are handicapped people out there can do things, can 'duct a meeting and can hold conversations, can do more things that other people cannot do."

I talked with Mark after the board meeting, a couple days after. Mark tell me, "People look up to you. You got power. You know how to do this and you got the know-how." Made me feel good inside; made me feel — well, somebody was supporting me.

And I never forget the day that Patty Sommers [an advisor — K.W.] says, "You are very tough. I don't know, you're just a tough person." Well I think she like how I conduct the meeting, how I said, "No, you can't to this; no, you can't do that. No, you got Step 1, Step 2, Step 3, Step 4." It was just something. Amaze, how I did it.

A board president has a lot of things to do, to keep focused on. We're bringing new ideas to the Board. The reports have to be right; policy has to be right; things have to be in order; you have to lay out the things for the Board of Directors.

My personal life changed a good bit. It helped me very a lot to understand myself, to understand people better, but I still had struggles with it sometimes. It was very, very hard path to follow, to get this together, be committed, and follow through what you're doing. I had to follow my own guidance. People tell me, "You didn't need no guidance because you already had it" — had guidance. I had a little bit. But it changed a whole lot for me.

It made me a lot busier. Made me go to chapter meetings, make sure that things was running right, running smooth, when I was president, and keeping on tap on Mark, making sure Mark got everything in order, making sure the records was taken care of, reports for the Board and stuff.

• • •

I talked to the people at Woodhaven. [a large state-owned institution — K.W.] They wanted me to come to their in-service. I told them about what Speaking For Ourselves is all about. I talked about how people abuse the system. I told 'em that we don't need to use shackles, because putting people in restraints does not help the matter, does not help the situation, at all. Throwing them down and holding them down — it doesn't help. You got to use other methods, other ways, to try to make the client understand the right from wrong. I thought I got my point across to them, to them officials, that these things needed to be straighten out, that people need to be out in a community. Because dollars are spent in an institution — every head is in an institution, a dollar is spent there and not in the community.

And where the dollar should be spent is in the community. The services need to be in the community and not in an institution.

Everybody really applaud and came up and told me that I did very good — told the things they want to hear. They told me no other person could stand there and say all that.

I went back and talked to people when the closing of the Pennhurst. But I didn't go back there to talk when people was still there; they didn't ax me.

I don't have preparation; I don't have a written paper or nothing in front of me. I just get up and say things that come, what's on my mind. I use things in my head; it just comes; I just use whatever comes out. I got this from the day program. I went out and spoke to some people, and that's how I got to speak more.

Mark does help other people; he lets them think about things themselves, then first he talks to them and then he gets them geared up: "Now remember what you say; make sure you say it plainly and sharper, so people can hear you clearly." He writes stuff out for them — those who can read.

I was scared when I was first going out and speak in front of people. It's like shy. What would I say to these people? What would I say to the county administrators? It was kind of scary. After I been doing it for a while, and kept doing it, I broke out of that shyness and keep focused on what I'm saying.

At the time I was working at Colmar, [a community mental health center — K.W.] before I went to Eastern College, St. David's. The director there said, "If you want to go, you can go, but you have to let your you boss know." So I let my boss know. I had to get things in writing and let them know two weeks ahead of time and then they let me off. Then I had some vacation time 'cumulated and so they let me take that, half of it. I remember getting the job at Eastern. We're out looking for a conference site. I told Mark that, "Hey, this is the place that used to be ARA and then they switched it over." They had a new food service company; it was Marriott. So I said, "Hold it, Mark, maybe I can get a job here. Maybe I can get my job back." I liked it so much. So I went in the back and I 'plied for the job and the boss called me the next day, "When could you start?" So I started the next day. I stayed there for five years. Colmar didn't want me to leave. I used to do maintenance; this was a day program. But I said I could not put up with that stuff — things happened to clients there that I seen with my own eyes: staff would hold a person down; it made me so upset; I just feel like I'm back in an institution.

Marriott was very hard to get off because my boss said, "You can't just go being traveling all over the ... — because I need you here." After I sat down and told him what I was doing to help people with disability, Ed was very pleased about this. And after that I got time off; he really took a lot of patience and time to work with me.

I have to get up early in the morning to get there at six o'clock. I have to take the bus from my house and get the subway and ride to City Hall and get the train to work. I had to walk pretty far. Took me three and a half hours. When it rained and snowed, it was just a hard struggle to walk in. I'd get home around 'bout nine or quarter to ten at nights. But I liked the place. My boss let me come in early and leave work early to go to board meetings. Ed Collins was understanding. Straight forward: "You have to be here on time. And if you don't, you don't get paid or I'm going to clock you out."

Somehow, I don't know, I convinced him he had to come to the Montgomery County ARC meeting. I told him, "This is something special." So he came. I got a reward and he heard me giving a good speech about employers hiring people with disabilities. And he was amazed about it. He says, "Gee. I had a good time at the banquet." He never been to anything like that. And he said that he would hire some people with disability. That was good. He said that I showed him that they could work as hard as anybody else had.

After when I came to be president the first time I travel anywhere to speak it was Erie. They wanted to hear about Speaking for Ourselves — "How we can get a chapter started out there in Erie, Pennsylvania?" So we went and spoke to them. We had to travel on a big plane and then we gotta go on the little plane. And I said the same thing: "How you could get a chapter started is you gotta find a founder, somebody like Luann, that is really want to dedicate themselves to being a founder." They would ax me how was I when I was a child: "How did you get active in Speaking for Ourselves?" and "What made you be part of Speaking for Ourselves?" And I told 'em that Speaking for Ourselves gave me a different outlook, appearance, in life. Yeah, we talked how do they get their people's rights and stuff like that.

I been to Canada. First time I met Bill Worrell and Patrick Worth [the advisor and one of the founders of People First of Canada — K.W.] they axed me to come out there.

When we went to Boston, I figured that I could travel by myself and learn to see the world, because I like to see little towns riding on the train and see what they look like, different cities and the different towns. It helped me to not be a-scared that there's nobody gonna be with me to show me how to get around. And it just ... It was a miracle. A miracle happened. Here I am — traveling by myself! And I can do it! I'm thinking about the other people driving on the van. This is one handicapped person less on the van. I was not afraid. I remember the train conductor told me the stop was the last stop you get off and there you are. I had somebody waiting and she picked me up at the train station with my luggage and stuff and drove me to the hotel.

Experiment. Yeah. I had a lot of experiments to run.

When they axed me to Interserv [a multi-state conference — K.W.] in Princeton, I was thinking so much, "What is going to come out of this — all these disabled people. I'm disabled. What do they see in me? What would they see in Steve? [Steve Dorsey, a Speaking For Ourselves Board member — K.W.] What is this all about?" I was kind of frightened about that. What do they see in us with disabled? What's this all toward? What it boils down to? And it was very, very hard to put the pieces together. It was like a puzzle.

I just thought, "Well, everybody here has a disability; I'm just like anybody else. My disability doesn't hurt anybody, because I'm a slow learner."

Then it was fun to watch, to see what was coming out of that conference. It was just people that had disabled, that they had something on their minds to tell people; they had something to say.

Speaking For Ourselves did an interview project at the ARC Rainbow at the workshop. We went in there as a paid consultant. We axed the clients did they like it in the workshop. Some said they did not like it in the workshop.

The person that I interviewed said, "Gee, I could fill out them questionaires."

I said, "Well that's what I'm here for, to help to fill out the questionaires. You can ax me the questions and I'll ax you the questions — what's on the questionaire."

So I axed him, "Do you think that you would like being in the workshop."

And he said No, he want a real job.

I think that Denver was the very first time that I flew to any of the professionals' conferences and back. Didn't bother me at all. Meeting all these people after we got off the plane ... Picked up a rent-a-car and then we went and checked in to our rooms. The next day it felt like that there wasn't no other disabled person here and we're the only disabled person here and fifty thousand TASH [The Association for People With Severe Handicaps — K.W.] professionals. It feeled like I didn't belong there. I felt like I didn't need to be there. It feel like that, "Gee, what do I have to talk about? What's on my mind to talk about in front of all these people?"

And it just came out: about make sure people getting their rights. We talked about how people with disabilities have different types of disabilities, about how we could make changes. Didn't worry me at all. Nothing worried me. I thought me and Steve brought out good questions and good answers. I think that me and Steve worked hand in hand too.

We went to Oregon and we spoke there how to get the chapters started. We was giving them advice. They was just starting to think about it — making things happen out there in Oregon. They axed us how did Speaking For Ourselves get started. We told them that Luann Carter was the founder and we had started out small and it grew and it developed a chapter in every county and been successful.

What inspired people ax me to come — because they thought that I had something to offer to them. They thought that I was a special person, that went out and did all this. I went to Wisconsin all by myself. They axed me to come and speak and I spoke and they said, "Gee, you talk like a very professional person. I never heard nobody talk as well as you talk." And it 'mazed me.

I would say, "Get people out of institutions. Make sure that people can get their rights. Stand up for the client; stand up for people's rights. Make sure that they get all that they can to better the system. And make sure that does not take place in other places — CLA's and group homes — because I been a victim to abuses in places."

I always had something to say. Whatever was on my mind, I would say it.

I would say, "Well, you can't treat clients like this. They have to be treated just … equal. They must be treated with fair and dignity. And you can't not have somebody tell them what to do. They have their rights, the clients have their rights too, like other people have, like you." And I kept saying that until I got it through to them. And it was very strong but I said it. And they heard. Even with the County of Mental Health and Mental Retardation. I did that with Steve [Steve Eidelman, Deputy Secretary for Mental Retardation for the Commonwealth of Pennsylvania — K.W.], made him understand that these the things you have to listen to. These the things you have to understand with clients. To make you aware of what the clients needs and what the clients want.

Well I have had this idea for a long, long time that I have seen people that mental retardation being treated awful in day programs and in group homes, in CLA's and boarding homes, where people been taken advantage of them. And they was not being treated fairly, the clients. I think they was being taken advantage. And that's how I got that; I think that's where I picked that up.

I think people with disabilities is being treated bad because the system, in itself, do not know how to treat people with disabilities with respect. In order to receive respect you have to give it and not take it. I mean treating people mean ... "You got to go to bed; you got to go here; you have to come in a certain time, have to be in the house, in the apartment, a certain time. If you not come in, I'm going to call the police; I'ma send the police after you." I think it's to scare you; I think that get people frightened that they're being watched by the system. And that's not respect, at all.

I think if it was worked right, I think the client would be a better; there would not be a lot of people being in psychiatric wards and being put back in institutions. I think if they was treated fairly and people sat down and talked to them in a nice way, they would not have this. I think the system would work good, if had better staff that would understand people they work and serve with them and not to abuse them and hold them down and tell them that they can't do this, they can't do that. If they want friends to come to see, girlfriends, they'll allow to have them. And that's not given to them. Staff would say, "Nope, can't have this; can't have this here. It's our program; you can't do it." So, that's what I mean by that. And that's what happens in these programs. I've been treated that way! And other people's been treated that way in the system. And this is true.

I don't think they are bad people; it was just how they're been trained. And if they was staff had been trained better, maybe they would have a better understanding with the clients and who they work with. I think things would work out smooth, if they was trained better.

I would tell them the same thing I'm telling now: that you can't treat clients cruelty; you can't treat clients nasty. If you treat the clients nasty, quite sure, the clients are going to treat you nasty. And if you want to treat them fair and nice, then the clients will treat you nice. I don't mean that every system in the system is going to work; I'm not saying that there are clients are hard to handle. And you have to use some kind of resources. But not holding down clients and putting them in places that they don't need to be put in. I feel that's very ... not right. It's not right. No, it's not right. The reason I say that is, it's the same way had been treated in an institution. If a person comes out of an institution, they say, "Well, this is my house. And if this is going to be my house, then I should run it like I should run it and not someone telling me what to do and how to do it." But some people don't have that authorities to say that, tell the staff, "This is my home. You working with me but you only come in and help me. You can't tell me what to do in my place where I stay and sleep." And that has been happening in a lot of them. Where I have been myself, been in that situation.

And sometimes I treat staff, if they didn't treat me well, I would treated them nasty. Not very nasty, but I would get upset. "Because you didn't treat me right, so I'll treat you ... . That's the way you want to be treated. I'll show you how I can act out. And if you don't not support me, I don't want you." So that's how I think the system is getting a little better.

There was people who treated me with some respect. And I treat them with some respect too. But there was some people you just couldn't get through, like people say. Every time I would have seizures, they think that I would put it on, act 'em. And they said, "Well, he's not really having seizures, just let him go." And it hurt me when they said that. I felt, in myself, "Why does staff say that, if they're supposed to be helping you?" They're supposed to be paid to helping you, to talk things out.

I can 'test for that in people's programs, some programs. I mean I been through all these systems that did not treat me like I wanted to be treated. And the same with boarding homes. They'll tell you, "If you don't act right in my house ... This is my house; you don't tell me what to do. You do what I tell you to do." And it was very hard to get people to understand that. I mean it's very hard for me to understand why they do that.

Up to this day ... Like for instance, I was living at Elwyn [a privately-operated institution — K.W.] and I stayed out. You have to be in at a certain time, a curfew time. Ten o'clock is your curfew; you can't be out now more late. So I stayed out late at eleven o'clock, way late, and it was past my curfew. The next day they told me, "How comes you didn't come in ten o'clock. You were supposed to be here at ten. Your curfew hour is that time." And sometimes you forget. And people, they treat you ... Why's you have to have certain curfew on you? Why they have to be in a certain time? Why can't they stay out from one to two? Why should they have to have all this curfew on them? I know that the system supposed to be looking out for their welfare, but it's kind of hard for clients to understand that.

It looks like to me it's a institution. "If you don't go by my rules here, then you have to move out, find another place. You don't like it here, you find an apartment." But you can still have somebody coming and telling you what to do in your own apartment. It's your apartment and you paid for it. Somebody's coming here and telling you what to do. And should not be that way. It's your apartment. You do what you do in your apartment once you sign that release. That's your apartment; you do what-ever you want to in your apartment. As long as you pay your electric bills and keep your laundry and your place clean and stuff like that, you won't run into no problems. So, that's what I think should happen. I'm talking because I've been in that same situation that everyone is.

• • •

I think that the name need to be changed. Our members do not like the name, "mental retardation." I think they're scared of that name. Because that means they're dummies; they're stupid persons; something like that. We're trying to get that name changed. I think it's a little discriminated that people call people mental retardation. They could say something else beside "mental retardation." A person has some kind of problems up in there, in their brains. But I don't think they should call it retardation. They should call it something else. Every time I go to conferences, there are people talk about that — that they don't want that name; they want it changed. But it's the ARC, the family, that wants to keep it that way. What the world'd be like — it'd be different. It'll be more that we are special people in some ways. But I don't think that other name should be called. We are special because we have a sense of our own; we know who we are; we know what we are doing; we got lots on the ball. You don't treat us like animals; we should be treated like adults.

It's people's struggle today — how to have an organization of their own. They get denied: people could not think that hand-icapped people could do this; that they need to be put away somewhere far away from us. That's where discrimination is coming. At one time they had not gave them a chance to express themself. Now things are changing. The government is looking at this in a different way. People are sitting with people with handicaps on boards in government. Before they never did this. This is what Dr. Martin King had really wanted — people to live happy lifes. The world would be different. And what I mean different — the world would be more nicer; people would understand us more better. When I say "us," I mean people with all kinds of disabilities; that they can't be discriminated against in this society that we live in. That would make me feel more happy. It would make other people feel better, not being discriminated against.

• • •

I was going out of some money and so I got 'em to get me to pay me $300 to pay my bills. And if I'm coming to speak, they're sposed to take me around. In Wisconsin they took me around the city and a famous restaurant where a lot of cowboys, Westerners, where they're dressed up in suits, like old-timers. It was very nice; I never seen anything like that. It was cold and we did some activities while we was there. We went to this big height and it was cold and we rode on a thing that rode back and forth — I don't know what you call it — but anyway, it was very nice in the mountains.

The first trip I went on at London, the People First International Conference, it was a very interesting. Oh, I enjoyed London! I never been to London.

This long ride ... I'm axed Mark, "We're still on this plane — how far is it?" 'Cause I usual in bed at this time and I'm still traveling.

And I said, "Mark, when this plane going to touch down?" My eyes was dozing off; I sleeped a little bit on the plane til Mark says, "We're here."

And it touched down at round 'bout quarter to eight, eight-fifteen of their time; three o'clock in the morning our time.

And I seen this daybreak.

Anyway, after we got in to London, we had to get our luggage and then we had to stop and get some pounds, their money, because I had traveling checks. And it was kind of hard for me to 'dentify what money from American money. I axed Mark, "What does that mean?" He 'splained it to me. It was kind of hard to 'dentify what is pounds, because I had no schooling about different countries. Well, anyway, when we got into the … it wasn't an apartment; it was like a dorms.

They invited me to come to learn more about our side. The next day they had their national meeting. And I got to stand up in front of all the people with disable. And I got up there and said that, "Now listen — you have to get together. If you want to form a international conference, we have to get it together. This is no joking matter. We have to concentrate on things that we have to do." That starred 'em up, everybody. I don't know how, don't ax me how I did it, but I did it. Yep.

It was very interesting to see how they accent talk; they talk different than I talk. And it was very powerful things that they said. We talked about how to get a self-advocacy organization started. It was a very powerful thing.

And then we took a tour. Me and Mark went on a bus and Bill Worrell. We went to visit Buckingham Palace and we went to see the Changing of the Guards and we ate in the park for lunch and we had a good time there. Bill Worrell had his self-advocacy group there from Canada — People First; it was a bunch of us.

It was a week; it went on for a whole week. We talked about some serious things up there. And it was very, very hard to imagine how that would work. Very hard to test that.

• • •

At Hershey Mark was saying, "You come down the hall. I has a surprise for you."

"A surprise? What kind of surprise? I don't like surprises."

And he told me to put the key in the door.

I opened the door and here's this big living room and with a big bed and the bathroom and the TV in the living room. It looked like for a big shot. I was shocked. I'm only one person. It was for a person that is a big shot, that had a lot of children; or three people could sleep in there.

And I was just, "Me? No, you must be kidding."

And he said, "Don't take this to your head."

There's a lot of people take things too serious to their head. But I don't take things seriously to my head.

It was very nice.

I think that was my end of my presidency. That's why they did that.

"Out!"

That's why they gave me that room. It was nothing put past me. I think that that's why that happened. Somebody set that up. Nobody told me. Everybody kept quiet.

It was a very, very good thing to do. It was very, very nice being in a suite at Hershey.

I had to say to myself, "Well, it's time to give other people a chance to be president. Because I can't be president all the time … " Giving them the chance to turn the gavel over to somebody else.

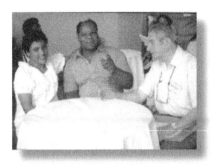

At People First Conference in Nashville,
August 30 — September 2, 1991
with Gunnar Dybwad and Debbie Robinson

At the signing of the ADA July, 1990
Washington, D.C., with Justin Dart,
Father of the ADA,
Ginny Thornburg, and Debbie Robinson,
fellow Speaking For Ourselves member

It kind of felt hurt inside, but it helped in the long run to give somebody else a chance.

It was very hard to give it up, very very hard to just say, "Well, I had it; I had enough of it" and give somebody else a chance in my shoes.

The board voted on whom will gonna be the next president. Debbie Robinson — she'll do the job in my place.

It's true I felt pushed out. It's kind of hard to put that together. I have no easy answers.

Debbie took the pattern and she followed the pattern: she was president, as I was president, in the Philadelphia chapter. She followed my lead. She picked up whatever I taught her. She learned what all from me.

And I got voted to a 'xectuive to the Board — making decisions for the Board.

And then I was elected back to president of Philadelphia.

They axed me to go to Pine Hill at that time to start a chapter in Pine Hill. [A small privately-operated institution for people with multiple disabilities, developmental and physical — K.W.] Bob Walsh [an advisor with Speaking For Ourselves — K.W.] invited me to come out there.

I went out there and took a look at Pine Hill, and I told Bob that he could not start a chapter in an institution. I better not hear him starting a chapter in an institution.

I talked to them about coming to the chapters, instead of having a chapter in Pine Hill. I told 'em that would not be right to start a chapter in Pine Hill because that if you start one, the staff would run it; the members wouldn't run it; it would be staff running it. It wouldn't be as good as other chapters would be. I told that the members had to come to the chapters and not have a chapter in Pine Hill.

I think that what would happen that it would not give the clients rights to do things for themself there. Because the staff would do it all for them, not the members themself. And that's been our policy in any chapter — that no staff was allowed in there while they're having their chapter meeting going on. It's been like that ever since. Because the members didn't like them to sitting in listening to what they're saying. Because like I said earlier they might take it back and tell, "They said something about us" and they will get on them saying that, "Why did you do that?" and they'll get punished for it.

I presented myself as a president.

"I'm Roland Johnson and I'm president at the Philadelphia chapter; I'm the one that runs the Philadelphia chapter meeting once a month and I would like to talk to you about our chapter. We meet Monday night once a month at Osteopathic Hospital. We sit around and talk about things, like's on peoples' minds. Speaking For Ourselves is a help-solve-problems organization. People speaks out, speak up for themselves. And it's un-profit organization."

I coax them to make them understand that this is right to come out of the institution. I told them about my life, how I was in an institution, how I was beated up. I told 'em my life first and then I talked about some of Speaking For Ourselves stories that helped me to understand things. And I would say that this would be a outlet for people to get out and help themselves, talk with themselves, with anything that they have on their mind. I said that this is the way you would get out of institutions — by coming to the chapters and showing yourself as a partner with Speaking For Ourselves. "We have to be united with one." I told them Speaking For Ourselves would make them feel self-fulfilled at the meetings that we have.

The thinking was behind that was to get people to be part of something that they believe; if they believe, really believed in, the people helping them, they have to be part of Speaking for Ourselves.

They listened to me and they all came. Bob started bringing people out to the Philadelphia Chapter. And then we would work with some people. Betty Brittingham wanted to get out of Pine Hill.

Big controversy over that — it really went on for two years. That they would come back each month and said, "Somebody is being abused up at Pine Hill." And they did not like it. They was not getting the things that they wanted.

So we went up there and we took a sneak attack — me and Debbie Robinson and Mark and Nancy and Judy Gran [Speaking For Ourselves' lawyer from PILCOP, Public Interest Law Center of Philadelphia — K.W.]; we went to see for ourselves if this was really happening.

And it was.

I saw the little babies crying, little infant babies; they was not being cared for right and they was howling and nobody came over to their rescue and they probably want their milk bottle. And we seen — actually I seen it with my own eyes — a staff person hit this lady in the bed — pinched her or something and she was crying. And Norm Baker [an advocate for people with disabilities — K.W.] went in there and axed her what she was crying about. And it really shocked me. It really brought a lot of the attention to Pine Hill.

It smelled like Pennhurst; it 'mind me of Pennhurst — the graffiti and the beds, just looked like Pennhurst. It was just a awful sight to see. How can anybody live in that kind of filth? I had tears when I came out of there. It was awful. And this is why we keep saying that we need to get people out of these institutions. Quick. They need to be out now. We need to keep people out of institutions; this is the things that we need to do. We have to face it. 'Fessionals have to face it. That these things are happening. And don't try to deny it. 'Cause it's happening in institutions.

I came out and I didn't like what I saw, so we went back to our chapter and we fussed about it. And then we got somebody to 'vestigate a little more and Judy Gran, our lawyer, 'vestigated and, of course, Norm Baker with his good seeing eye opened his mouth and called Steve [Eidelman — K.W.] and worried Steve.

And Norm Baker said, "This is happening! It needs to stop. You need to come up here and look at it yourself."

So, that's what happened. I think he got his other people and went up there and looked at it. It went a year, one year, until we got people out of there and into a community and into other places. They got new people to come in and a new director.

Betty Brittingham got out; we helped her get out of Pine Hill and several other people up there. About half are still there. And we're still looking for more people living out of there.

And then they had big advocacy, but I did not take part of it: I couldn't get off, I was working out in Eastern College at St. David's. I wanted to be there, but I just couldn't find the time to be there.

• • •

I was elected president of the Board again, but I didn't want it no more, 'cause my body couldn't take it. The pressure was too much for me; president's role was too much. I was sick. I had colds, cold after cold, and 'monia. I just couldn't run the president anymore. So I had to give it up.

I didn't do much. I was on the national steering committee; they votes me as a national steering committee in Nashville, to help people where to go, how to set up the next meeting.

I resented President Bush with a plaque, a reward for the ADA.

I was interviewed on CNN.

I lecture with Nancy Nowell — that was a job for CHC [Coordinated Health Care — K.W.]

We got people out of Embreeville — some of them, they're not all out. [A state institution which has now been closed — K.W.]

I talk to case managers in county offices about how to handle people when people come out of institutions, not to treat them mean or bad, because they can get very violent and you don't want to put them back in the institution; I don't want to see them back in the institution. I told them living in an institution was a horriful place; people beat you up; it was horrible.

• • •

I kept on believing and praying and hoping that this book will be written for people's 'sideration, letting people know about my life story. I thought of it — I said that this book might be written, if I can find someone to help me to write the book. I'm a person that believes that something is going to happen. And it will take place; it will. I had no doubts in my mind that it would not never happen. It will happen.

This book is a story about my life; it's about my whole life story from now to then.

~ The End ~

Roland Johnson presenting
President George Bush with ADA Award,
January 12, 1993
(official White House photograph)

Roland Johnson at the 1994 ADA Award Ceremony
(President Bush speaking)

APPENDIX: PUBLIC SPEAKING

. . . .

December 9, 1987 WHYY-FM Philadelphia:
Interview with Marty Moss Cohane
(excerpt)

Roland Johnson: ... I think back in them days that they didn't have no kind of choice what to do with their child. Years ago they said that these people are not fit for society. "Get them away from us because they would try to harm us and what should we do with them." But is it always going to be putting them back in an institution, put them down, or put a label on them or something? I feel that should not be. I keep thinking like that. Now things are changing. But not much. We're working on it; we're working towards it. Speaking For Ourselves, the organization I'm involved with ... I can just only touch on this ... Speaking For Ourselves is involved with a lot of closing down of Pennhurst. Speaking For Ourselves has been a private, un-profit organization that's been in the system for five years. We just went through our five years anniversary this year. It has been talking about people, cursumers, don't need to be put into an institution. And at conferences that we been to, they don't want to take the label off of mental retardation. And I feel that Speaking For Ourselves is a strong will power to try to look at this thing. With the human services and the help of the people in general as a whole. We're all into this together. We need to look at this more strongly. And work together as a unit. To change ideas.

The way that people see us. Not the way they see us from years back. Look up from now. Are we going to continue working and living as people put us down that we aren't not fit for the outside? I don't think so. We have come this far. Why should we go back? I feel that we have came through a very strong little test. I think it's a testing for us. How long can it go on? How long until the mental retarded and disabled can be left out in the community for services?

Marty Moss Cohane: I think that many people on the outside think of institutions closing, and then they think of street people. They think of people living on vents or in parks and having no place to go. When we hear about the closing of a place like Pennhurst, I suppose the idea is that people will just be roaming and not be able to take care of themselves. And then the fear that they would hurt themselves or somebody else then rises to the top. But you live in an apartment and you have a roommate and you have someone who checks in on you about once a week to see how things are going.

RJ: Right. A team or the county office or the group where you're staying makes the decisions. That's made up of individuals. If maybe there's something going wrong there — someone couldn't get along with his roommate or something — then a change has to be made, to be placed somewhere else.

MMC: What do your neighbors think of you? Do you have much contact?

RJ: I wish we did have a lot of contacts with our neighbors. But our neighbors don't even know that we're there hardly.

MMC: Well you're working ...

RJ: One neighbor who lives upstairs from us, she said, "Well we don't hear no noise, no racket." I play my radio or TV. It's just like a normal person. You're just a normal person like anybody else.

MMC: The reason I ask is that I think a lot of people have a lot of crazy ideas about living next to someone who's different from themselves.

RJ: Oh they do. They think, "What's he doing out here by himself instead of being monitored? Because we got kids around, we got children around. What's going to happen to our children? Is he going to hurt them?" This is what 'volves. This is what happens. But I don't think that's going to happen by the help and strength of the people, by sharing and caring with support each other. And I think that with staff, what I mean, not staff there all the time ... But with minimum supervision, not there all the time to tell us what to do, but just keep an eye, close eye on you and come and check perialically. If things are going on all right, they don't need to be there. Because they got a lot of other people that needs more services than others. And I think that by giving the person that can do things for themself just a little assistance, and give it to someone else who might be more quote mentally retarded. You hear on radio talk shows that people sleeping out on the streets. In the back of my mind I'm wondering — is there services there for them also? We want to correct that confusion.

MMC: I think you raise a really good point which is that people just don't understand the distinctions between different groups and the kinds of problems perhaps people might have. It sounds like what you're saying is that the street people really kind of cast a bad shadow on you and people like you who are working.

RJ: We want to make sure that we are not the only ones is benefitting by it and getting all these services and they are not getting services — the blind, the disabled.

MMC: I regret to say that we're out of time and I feel like we've just gotten going, but I do thank you so much for talking with us today.

RJ: I thank you for being here. It's a pleasure.

March, 1993 (2) Workshops for Self-Advocates
At "Everyday Lives" — Annual state-wide Conference in
Hershey, PA
sponsored by the Commonwealth of Pennsylvania

FINDING A VOICE

Finding a voice to me is finding somebody that is going to really speak up for people with disabilities and with handicaps; who serves the system; who is in the system; and who will come to be for working in the behalf of starting a group around the world.

What it is to me: finding a voice is to make things happen; make things really happen, that it is going to happen with people with disabilities.

... Not to be shy. We want to know — how can we help you to get what you want from us and what we want from you. We want you to talk up — please. Not to be shy.

Now some of you people came to our retreat at Fellowship Farm and you told us that you want to start a group in Pennsylvania. But we want you to talk up — don't be afraid. Talk up ... [give and take with the group ...]

STARTING A CHAPTER

... and what it took to start a Philadelphia chapter. When I was chapter president, it was very hard for me to start and for people to listen. We started our chapter at the Girls High at Broad and Olney in Philadelphia in Pennsylvania in Philadelphia. They had night school there and the principal came around with a note and said that there was a chapter meeting downstairs in the kitchen. So I was very interested in being a chapter president, helping to make Speaking For Ourselves go — I was very interested in being part of that. And I been a part of it for five years ... So that's how it got started ... [give and take with the group ...]

Hello. Can I hold the mike, please?

I am going to do a role play here. I'm going to ax you — you listen very carefully — I'm going to ax you where you from and where you live — this is just a little test — and what state you from ...

My name is Roland Johnson. Glad to meet you. I am a chapter president and there's some things that I want to know from you ...

[give and take with the group ...]

I would like to involve you all into the chapter meeting. And I'm going to start off by saying my name: My name is Roland Johnson and I live in Philadelphia, Pennsylvania. And people come to our chapter at the Osteopathic Hospital at City Line Avenue. They meet once a month at City Line Ave. And I would like to get some ... I'm gonna ... Let's make pretend you at City Line Avenue and you the members of the group.

Now I'm gonna ax the group ... Some of you are new ... I don't know none of you; I don't know anything about you. So I want to know something about you — where you live and what you do and what's going on. So I'm going to ax ...

[to first person ...] What brought you here ... what got you involved? Do you mind speaking up? ... Did you bring a friend? ... Tell me something about yourself ...

[give and take with the group ...]

[first issue ...] Matthew, my name is Roland Johnson; glad to meet you. First of all you have an issue and I want to help you with that issue. You want to tell me something about the problems that you have? Tell the group ... What have you know about the chapter? Has the chapter helped you? ...

I think that's a very nice thing to do [cookie sale to raise money — K.W.]. But I want to know if you involved everyone in your group ... So you all baked and that's how you got to come here by raising money ...

... New members cannot speak for themselves and you can get these people involved. Involve them all what you live at, where they live and stay — so they can be involved too, because they might have problems to deal with to come to the chapter. How do you get people to get involved in your county? Well, what we did was send little cards, 4 by 4, with your name and your company or whatever — where you're from — put your telephone number on the card; we send like a little registration card ...

[introducing Luann Carter, founder of Speaking For Ourselves — K.W.] She's gonna tell it in her own words — I'm not gonna talk for her. She's a person that very dedicated for what Speaking For Ourselves ... and very hearted dream-wise. I think she's a dream-woman; she's a dreamer. And the dreams that she came up with — it was a long time ago ...

[Luann speaks ...]

Thank you Luanne with that 'spiring words and efforts.

I would like to say some groups are ... Sometimes staff are in control of your groups and that sometimes takes away what you're trying to do. I think it's a good idea that staff is not a advisor; I don't think you can use staff as advisor because it takes away for what you're trying to do and what you're supposed to be doing and looking for. Now advisors are there for to help you to make things happen ... when you get stuck ... or things that you can't not do. That's what an advisor role is. Advisor role is: Who's in control. I wanted to know who's in control because you are the people is running your chapter and running your groups. Because if you get too many staff person try to run the group they try to take over. And that's one thing you can't let do — let staff persons take over. But an advisor's role is to sit back and try to help you be individual. To help the president and the vice-president and the secretary and whatever. The advisor role is to maintain your chapter. The president is to maintain order in the chapter and maintain a kind of a system with other people. The other part is to help people to make people understand that you are in control; you are in control to run your meetings the way you want to run it and not the staff. The advisors are there to help you when you get stuck in things. And the reason why I know this because I been the chapter president 'fore I came to be a Board President. And what that is it's a very hard task to be a president, taking on a role of responsibilities over a chapter. If somebody's trying to take over, there's no sense in needing a chapter if you're not in control over the chapter that you serve. Thank you.

114

APPENDIX: PUBLIC SPEAKING

March 3,1993 Workshop: "HIV/AIDS: Practical Approaches
to Prevention and Service Delivery" at
"Everyday Lives" state-wide Conference
sponsored by the Commonwealth of Pennsylvania
[assisted by Nancy Nowell]

I'm a member of Speaking for Ourselves; I'm a part of the
Speaking for Ourselves, making things happen that people will
get their life more better. With Speaking for Ourselves we have
members do things for their everyday life, like coming to boards
and 'powering other people to make their life change different.
And my life is part of their life.

At one time I used to be part of an agency with a lot of
other people, a big agency, North Central. And after North
Central phased out, Comprehensive phrased in; then after
Comprehensive phased out then part of Colmar took over. And
I was shuffled in lots and lots of places. They did not make my
life more happy; it did not make my life more safe.

At that time — in '73, I think, if my memory serves me
correctly — at that time I was in the hospital and I remember
that Peggy L. had came and told me that, "Did you know North
Central is closing?" And that, "We have to move you, shift you
around, shift people around again?" I didn't like it so much,
but people just don't understand the system. It should make
the system better by listen to the consumer, the people that you
serve, better.

I come from a lot of backgrounds. I used to live at Elwin;
I don't like that name so much. But I used to live at Elwin at
Chestnut Hall, 40th and Market. I came through from a tough,
tough start — a tough situation. And after all this moving

around and shifting around that we did with other agencies and shifting around with all the clients, I don't think that was a fair idea to do.

Now the issue that I'm up here for is to make sure you people empowered about the HIV. And I would like to know:

How many people that served in the MR system?

Show of hands ...

Who works for the system, in the MR?

Quite a few of you ...

Who works with people in the agencies, the caretakers? Anybody?

Well, I would like to see that. I thank you for showing your great efforts.

But we don't stop there. Our great efforts do not stop there.

My issue is: I was HIV positive; I have HIV, but I don't have AIDS. I've been knowing that I have AIDS for five, five and a half?

[Nancy Nowell: Maybe four years ...]

Four years. The reason I'm turning to Nancy: Nancy Nowell is my support and she knows all about the history, as well as I do.

[N.N.: Tell them what it feels like ...]

What things feels like, when people that have HIV — they forget things, they don't remember things that happened to me. I am taking all different types of medicine that would help me to sleep at night; sometimes I have sleeping nightmares, that somebody has to be with me every other night because I wake up and I think that there's somebody after me.

I know a friend named Chuck W.; Chuck had HIV; he had AIDS. And I don't want to take part of this time and talk about him ...

AIDS is very, very ... a bad disease — you don't think of AIDS as bad disease. When the doctor didn't tell me that I had AIDS, when he test my blood level, when he tested things and I questioned him on things about AIDS — do I have HIV — he never told me that I had AIDS. And I was kind of very scared when he didn't tell me that I had AIDS. Then I went to another doctor to find out did I have AIDS.

Yes, I have another doctor, Dr. Gross, Maurice Gross. He tested me for HIV, because I didn't feel like I was comfortable back ... Hey — I had AIDS. "You have AIDS." I had to find out for myself from another doctor. "Would you please tell me the truth: Do I have AIDS; do I have HIV positive?" So they tested me again and got my records from Philadelphia and they said that ...

How this all happened, I came to talk with Mark Friedman ... I don't like to name names because the person could get into troubles; I'll get into troubles. He was the one who had followed me through with the doctor in Philadelphia. Sometimes the doctors don't understand, because he was just learning about, probably, about HIV. So I had found another doctor from Abington Hospital; he's a private doctor. I possibly had AIDS. Possibly. I wasn't satisfied yet. Till I had to sit with Carole Nettleton; she's a very special counselor; she's a specialize in different fields. And I had axed Carole Nettleton again, "Do you think that I have AIDS? HIV?"

She said that, "You don't have AIDS, but you have HIV."

Now, two different things can happen in people's lives, with two people. By not using safe sex, the proper ways of using safe sex — it is had to happen. People have to know that. The people that you are supposed to be serving don't have that chance to have what other people want — have to have.

Have sex ...

But the right way to have sex is use a condom. To demonstrate a condom we have some things over here after I get done. I think that people need to understand that people are no better off. Instead of saying, "You can't have sex. It's wrong. It's very wrong." I think people should have sex, because that helps to stim themselves. But in the right way.

I want to know why the people that you're serving are not allowing to have sex. Because sex is the heart of their inside. You take that away and tell them and say, "Well, you can't have sex." What are you going to do? Just open our minds, open our understanding, that these people that they serve, these people have been in institutions, trying to date girls and trying to have girlfriends, but they come out of an institution and they said, "Oh, you don't do this in my program. I'm not allowed that. You do not do this in our program."

I went to Elwin and they have strict rules; I couldn't understand their rules. Their rules is that "You do not bring a person in this place without us knowing about it. You want to do that stuff, you do that stuff on the outside." Where's the place to go to do it? You can't do out in the street; that's in public; that's a very nasty place to do it. People have to understand that you have to open up and let these clients ... — they're clients that you're serving.

I have been doing this for quite a while without condoms, because I never knew about any ...

It's hard for me to make this point out.

How many of you know of people in your program that have relationships with girlfriends and you tell 'em, "Not here. Not do that. Don't do that. It's not allowed."

How many? How many?

I want a show of hands ...

How many?

Quite a few ...

Who makes these laws? Who writes them?

Nobody.

It's time now to let go and let the clients be aware of what they're doing. Because that's how they get frustrated; a lot of strustrated come from people that don't allow them to do what they want to do. Because the thing is — this person wants to have a date, a relationship. He don't know how to give back to people; no one has taught him.

Another thing — I was in Pennhurst for ten years. And I was a child at Pennhurst. I have been sexually abused by another client, a patient up there. And I couldn't understand why this 'lowed, this stuff to go on. And that's what happened; that's how I picked it up. He picked it up from other people. I was no more that eight years old when I went there.

And it is a shame; people think that's a shame, very nasty: "You're filthy."

Why?

You all have some kind of relationship with people.

They're human. They're human. Maybe they can't get their point of view across, but they understand. They wonder; they see other people do it; or their mother do it; their mother and father do it. And so they pick that up from, maybe, when they was babies. I understanding from another person that you learn that as you was a child. And don't let nobody in this room tell me you don't think they don't pick that up as you're growing. You do.

I was in Pennhurst and I couldn't push this guy away from me. It was hard; I was hurt. "I don't want to do that." People need to understand and waking up the system — because people need to hear about this. This is nothing that you can go away from it; can't hide it. It's out there. Many years ago in the gay community it was locked behind the doors, closed behind the doors. And people said, "Well, I'm going to hide myself in the door because I don't want my identity ... So I'll lock myself in the door." Now it's coming wide open.

When you touch somebody with AIDS, you can't get it.

You can't get it by taking hands.

You can't get it by kissing or you can't get it from the toilet, from eating off or dripping out of somebody's glass.

You can only get this from contacting with another person's ... with a female or a male.

And the reason why I had gone to an AIDS course training at Temple University — and I think I passed that course — people came from New Jersey to teach us.

I want to ax another question: Who works around people that have AIDS?

Anybody?

[N.N.: Everybody.]

Everybody. Everybody.

Are you scared of them? Are you afraid to touch them?

If you're not scared to touch them, and you work around with them everyday, are you going to catch it? Why? I understand people wear gloves ...

[N.N.: We're going to talk a little bit about prevention and other stuff ... Can I ask you two questions that I think only you can answer? 'Cause they're real important. How did it feel when you started to tell people you're HIV positive?]

How did it feel that I was HIV positive?

Unhappy.

[N.N.: No — when you started to tell people.]

When I started to tell people?

[N.N.: How did they react to you?]

Um, I went out and tell that I am AIDS, HIV — I keep getting the AIDS and HIV mixed up — I went and told my sister about that I have AIDS, that I have HIV. When they heard about that I had AIDS, they got very scared; they got very bent out of shape. "Don't you come and tell me that you have AIDS! I don't know what you do! Don't ... "

I figured that they was gonna say, "Don't come near me; I don't want no parts of you. You know what the Bible said about this, about having sex with another man."

Oh, I was very unhappy about it. But I had several other people helping me with this. It was a partnership: that person went with me to my house — Mark Friedman and Dr. Carol Nettleton — went to my sister's house and I introduced to all my sisters. And I had thought I couldn't do this alone because it was very scary; I didn't know how to present this with people by myself, so I had to have a partner, a couple partners, to help me to do this.

My oldest sister said that she was with me. "I'll stand and support you. As long as your body is strong, well ... " And every time I go somewhere, every time she's hearing I'm going to Harrisburg, going to Washington, she said, "Well, your body must be feeling well, because you're going, you're doing all these things that anybody else that has AIDS can't not do" — cannot do all the things that I could do.

But there's another side to this. I'm taking AZT. AZT helps the immune system to build up the white cells count. Sometimes

I'm afraid to take the medicine because the medicine makes me lose concentration; I can't think. But I have to take it, if I want to get better. I have to take the medicine if I want to get better. I do want to get better. But it's hard to make people to understand that people need to hear this in the mental health field. People need to hear this and not to play games with it. You can't play games with the clients that you're supposed to be serving. I don't understand why people don't like to be working ... See when I go outside, I can hear people say, "Oh look at that man walking up there. He might have AIDS. Stay away from him." But to me it's just like anything in the book: I got AIDS. So what. I got HIV. So what.

[N.N.: Tell them what happened at your job. Tell them about your job.]

I had a good boss. I used to work at Eastern College at St. David's out in the suburbs. And Ed Collins was my boss. And he was the sweetest boss that I ever worked for. And when I talked about my health going down, that my body was not feeling well, he said to me, "What's going on with your body?" He called me in his office, shut the door, and me and him had private conversation with each other. Me and him converted together. And Carol Nettleton and Mark Friedman was doing that with me, to make him understand, make him aware that I had HIV. He said, "Oh, does he? What can I do for him? I'm willing to do anything for him." He did not say, "I'm going to get rid of him, just because he has AIDS, got HIV." Because my other supervisor had HIV too. But it was getting too much for me; it was taking out too much under pressure ... Washing pots, standing on my feet all day, and I was getting kind of tired and worn out. So I went to him and I said, "It's time for me to change over for another job." "Why?" he said, "Why? Why are you changing over your job? I understand what you got. I'm pleased, I'm happy to have you here to work for me." "But Ed, I have to change over to another job." And the job that I changed over — I love that job so much; they treat me like a person — with dignity. Carrol Reckard [Administrator in Ken-Crest Center's Family Living Program — K.W.] and her husband Willie watches out for me. She has her head down, but she really works hand in hand with me to deal with that.

I never forget: from Elwyn when they heard that I had AIDS — let me tell you — when they heard that I had HIV, they said, "Well, I don't think we can serve you. I don't think you can stay here, because we don't know how to deal with it." They was ready to throw me out in the street. And I said, "They're are people supposed to help me? To serve me? And they're getting money to help me and they're trying to pitch me out in the street?" And I think this happens in ... It might not be happening all the programs ... People are in the mental health field, mental retardation field: that people don't need to be treated that way. "If you can't have AIDS, we can't take care of you." That's wrong. That's wrong. People need to understand that they special people, people that needs care for, need to understand. You have a thousand people living in this Philadelphia area who sleeping down in the subway. They probably have AIDS and they don't know it. People need to go and get tested for HIV. People need to understand that this is very serious.

With this close, I think, Nancy's going to share some of that with you. Because my 'lectric friend is running out here. I'm glad that you all came to hear; I hope that you heard something; I hope that you are got something out of this little bit. If anything that you want to ax me, you can do so. But I would prefer me her talk together, hand in hand, because she understands; she knows the backgrounds of me and she knows a lot of things that I don't know. I'm being honest! ...

At Speaking For Ourselves Annual Conference
May 15, 1993

At Speaking For Ourselves Annual Conference, Delaware
County Community College, with Nancy Thaler,
Pennsylvania Deputy Secretary for MR

Speaking For Ourselves Annual Conference
May 15, 1993
Delaware County Community College, Pennsylvania

You know me: I'm always on time; I like to get things on time, have smooth on time so things can go smoothly. Can I put this mike up a little? I would like to get things started. I'm going to ax the people from out there to please come in so we can get started. I know it's not ten o'clock yet but we want to be on time. I would ax no one to be moving around while I'm on the podi ... While I'm up here; nobody's to move around.

I must say that as your master of ceremony today — we have good things in store for you.

I know there's still more people coming in ...

Also we have a special guest today. Is Bob Perske around? Can he come to the podium, please? Bob Perske?

We would like to get started; it's almost ten o'clock. I don't know about your watch, my watch says five of ten. And we want to get started.

I want you guys to say, out there in the audience, "Welcome!" Shake hands with your co-workers. And welcome to our twelfth, eleventh year conference.

I am still looking for Bob Perske. Is Bob Perske in this building? Would you all quiet down please!

[another voice: Quiet! Quiet! Shh!]

Bob Perske? (Nancy, is Bob Perske out there?)

I want you all to say with me, "Good morning!" How are you? Are you going to have a good day today? Well, well, I want you to shake hands with your partners. And say, "How are you doing today?"

With that introduction, we're going to start off. Jerome, Judy Gran come in please.

We're going to recognize people here today. I'd like to tell you, first of all ...

If you take out your program for today, if you got your book, if you got your folders, please take out your program today. And the first one is the agenda ... I would like to say at this time and introduce at this time some county representators and some state representators. And we are very happy to have our state representators from each county, representing each county individually.

First of all we want to give thanks to our, to our moderator for today, for this afternoon, will be taken part of the moderator for this afternoon. I'm up here this morning, and I will be back with you this afternoon again. Our moderator is on my left side, for this afternoon. And Zach is on, is going to be the interpretator ... sign, for today. Zach. This is Zach. Everybody, say, "Zach."

I want you to say, "Good morning, Nancy Thaler." [Deputy Secretary for Mental Retardation for the Commonwealth of Pennsylvania — K.W.]

I want you to say good morning to Nancy Thaler's husband, he's going to lead us into — not yet — but he's going to lead us into a song and Debbie Robinson is going to help to lead you into the song.

It gives me the pleasure to introduce to my friend and my colleagues ...

I been knowing Bob Perske for a long, long time. Bob Perske has been a founder and a helper, for supporter, of Speaking for Ourselves ...

(I'm looking for a Bob Perske book ...)

Bob Perske writes books about people, different people, and their lifes, and equal justice and that's what he's for. This book, that you can buy off of us, half-price — I don't know how much is the half-price, but I got told that this book is a half-price. And you can buy this book by Bob Perske. He's a very good, strong man and he believes in things that we believe in. By getting people out of institutions and standing up for people's rights and standing up for the justice — one of the persons had went to prison ... I think I'd better let him tell you that on him.

Now, Bob Perske's been working in an institution, volunteer in an institution ...

And here he is ... I'm going to give him a ... while you give a good welcome, a round of applause for Bob Perske. Bob is going to speak for ten minutes. And if you look on the side, on the page, you can pull out the page on Bob Perske, what he does. Thank you.

[Bob Perske speaks ...]

Now, okay, thank you.

Now I would like to present Karl Williams and Debbie Robinson is going to lead you into a Speaking for Ourselves song.

[The song: "Speaking For Ourselves" ...]

I am not going to let Karen Snyder get away from us just quick. [Secretary of the Department of Public Welfare for the Commonwealth of Pennsylvania — K.W.] She is a very, very understanding person. And her first time here, being here with Speaking for Ourselves. We're the ones who's got her here ... had got her here to understand about Speaking for Ourselves. I think she knows that already. But in her own words she might have tell us something about what Speaking for Ourselves do. We don't want her to be sit 'tentively — we want her to come and be part of us with Speaking for Ourselves. She has a big top job on her — she is Nancy Thaler's boss. She is fighting in your behalf of speaking out for ourselves. And she is a dear lady to us — to have her here, this morning, to be with us, today. And it is my pleasure to, to have her stand up, and Karen Snyder, to let everybody know who Karen Snyder is. She's the director of MH/MR in Harrisburg. I have been to her conference and she has taught me something; she knows a whole lot of things and we appreciate you for coming today, being part of us. I hope that you could stay around for the whole day. Debbie's going to take her around and show her college while she's here. Thank you.

With that we're going to move on.

Now we're going to go to classrooms. Now listen up! Listen up, that what I'm going to say. Everybody have a colored dot on your name tag? That's the colored dot that you will ... that's the class that you will be in. The first class.

Don't move anywhere — not yet!

Sit down — not yet!

[Further directions and people move out ...]

Third International People First Conference
Toronto 6/93

[Debbie Robinson's introduction.]
Thank you. Thank you, Debbie. I'm glad to be here today. I'm
very glad to be here at all this three days. Today we're gonna
talk about: How to be in control; who's in control. I want to
know — raising hands — who are in control.

Are you in control?

Are staff in control?

Well, I understand that you need to be in control, and some
of them are not in control because staff tells you what to do;
advisors tell you what to do and staff tells you what to do. I
don't believe that you are in control over your life. And there's
some people out of state needs to understand that you are — the
people are — 'posed to be in control of your life: how to set up,
how to do things, how to make people understand you, how to
make people love you and care for you.

I come back in Pennsylvania, I speak in front of a hundred
people in Philadelphia.

My name is Roland Johnson and I'm glad to being here for
welcome you here.

Control means being in self-control ... who's in charge over
you.

Are you in charge?

Is staff in charge?

But who's in charge?

Well, some people tell me that sometimes staff is in control,
that you don't be in control over your life. And doing things
in your workshops or in day program and in where you live —
staff in control.

I want to know who is telling you what to do. If you're telling yourself what to do or are you letting staff tell you what to do.

I can't hear you!

You're supposed to be in charge, right?

I can't hear you!

Who's in charge?

All right.

Are the workshop people in charge?

How about people getting the jobs?

How do you go to your supervisor or your staff, that you want to get a real job and work in community and on real jobs? How do you do that?

Can anyone tell me how you do that?

[Voice.]

You go to your people whenever you want?

[Voice.]

You tell them what you want. But do they listen?

[Voice.]

Are they supposed to be serving you? I think that they sometimes want to take control. And people are not supposed to be taking in 'trol; staff is not taking in control. If this is supposed to be a movement — I think that you supposed to be in how to tell them what you want done. And how to do things. And how to tell them, "Get off my back; let me be in charge; let me have in control over my life!"

I don't know how to put it this way, but I understand that there are a lot of people sometimes are not in control over their life; are not saying to themselves and saying to staff, "I want to be in charge of my own life. I want to be in charge."

Can you say that? With me?

I want to be in charge over my own life.

Not you telling me what to do.

I want to be in charge of my own life.

And I have a lot of people tell us that sometimes people just don't listen. There're people out there doesn't really listen to you. I know in Pennsylvania they don't listen very hard, very nicely. So we have to waken people up and make people understand that we are in control of our own life and tell us what to do. 'Cause when I was in Pennhurst, Pennhurst State School, I had people who controlled my life. I had people control me and tell me what to do, tell me when to get up, tell me when to go to bed, tell me what not to do: "If you don't go to work, if you don't do the things that you're supposed to do, then your privileges will be taken away from you."

How many people be in a situation like that? Show of hands.

Quite a few. Quite a few of you have been in situations like that, just like me.

How many people have been in programs that tells you: "You can't do such-and-such a thing; you can't do it here, not here, not in here." Show of hands.

Good.

And the only way to break that barrier is to tell people that you are in control. You are in control over your own life and in your own ways. And tell people — be honest and be sincere — and say that: "I am in control over my life; not you tell us what to do and how to control your money and how to control who's in control." And that's what I go around the country saying: "Who is in control?"

I been at London, England 'bout three years ago and I said the same thing and I got the very round of applause, clapping: Who's in control? Because sometimes people think that you can't do it; you can't do the things that you're 'posed to do. They don't trust you enough. If you be honest enough that they might trust you, if you do the things that you're supposed to do.

I mean every day that you live in your program, that they're not supposed to tell you how to make changes come. How to make people listen to you?

Listen — listen: is two different things. Listen and telling somebody what to do is two different things. And it's hard to listen to, to understand people.

I'm not going to take up too much of your time. I'm gonna just say: Thank you for this, for me to come here and speak. I'm want to give honor to Patrick Worth for allowing me to come here and speak to you and for all this week. Thank you very much.

February 1, 1994 West Chester, PA In-service training for
case workers of people who once lived in institutions
[with Susan Bartholomew]
(excerpts)

... As I was saying, I'm from Speaking For Ourselves and I do a
lot of things with Speaking For Ourselves. We try to get people
out of institutions and stuff like that. We go sit on PAC [Planning
Advisory Committee: a group consisting of consumers, parents,
providers, advocates, and state and county government officials which advises the Office of Mental Retardation of the
Commonwealth of Pennsylvania on policy matters — K.W.], the
DD Council [Developmental Disabilities Council — K.W.], the
Steering Council [a group elected to organize a national self-advocacy organization — K.W.], and a lot of different types of
committees I sit on. And the reason for that is just to give my
opinions about people being in institutions. I was in an institution before at Pennhurst, because I had some problems with my
mother and my mother couldn't handle me at the time anymore
and so I was under a court case designed to go to Pennhurst.
Looking for a way at Pennhurst ... Running away from home ...
Running away from my mother at home ...

[Susan Bartholomew: Can I say something about some other
things around I guess, Speaking For Ourselves. I didn't get to
completely introduce you. You've been a very active member
there for maybe about nine or ten years; you've been the past
president of the Philadelphia chapter, past president of the
Speaking For Ourselves Board. Roland's been very active, as he
said, speaking in the communities. He doesn't talk about this,
but he's met President Bush. You gave him an award. You went
to the ADA signing in Washington.]

Me and Debbie Robinson watched the president signed the ADA.

[S.B: And you've spoken in London ...]

I went to London three years ago and spoke there with three thousand people there and spoke about how to get a chapter going there in their country. And they wanted to hear me so much that everybody stood up and gave me a round of applause. (He laughs.)

It takes me a while to get started to talk about how people being in institutions ... I was in an institution at Pennhurst. Pennhurst was horrible; it was very very very horrible there.

Looking at the situation there: people used to be being hit there. I was put there under the age of ten years ...

[S.B asks questions and Roland responds ... Conditions at Pennhurst when he was there.]

It's horrible to talk about something like this, people being in institutions. With the lot of patients there that they had there at Pennhurst, I think it was kind of hard for them to manage a lot of people with handicap disabilities ...

Have you ever been out to Pennhurst? Have you heard of an institution like Pennhurst? Byberry State Hospital? Embreeville? Have you? Well that's some of the things that goes on in an institution. And this is why I keep discussing about people being in institutions, because things can go wrong, things can happen to them, and people can be hurt and be injured and different things. Like little kids can be very abused — sexual abuse. They was some sexual abuse going on out on D-4; there was some very crime, bad bad behavior pattern; and attendants didn't do anything about it. You go and tell the attendant; the attendant says, "I have nothing to do with it." Their hands was tied. So, what happens is that you tell the head supervisor and all she would do is write up conduct reports and send it in to L college and you had to go over there and meet the superintendent the next morning ...

What made it a bad experience? If you went out there today and seen Pennhurst today, and if they had people today up there, you would say to yourself, "Do I want my son and daughter there? Is this how they treat you? In filth and roaches crawling down on the walls and bugs and mouses running in the wards. It was horrible. I don't think that the superintendant had anything to do with it; he had his hands tied. I think the people that managed the money didn't look at the place very well — what needed to be done; what needed to be fixed up; and what needed to be taken care of. It was not a good management care. I can sit here today and tell you and keep telling you: It was not the way it should be. Now in the hospital it was management care very well. Very well. But the wards was not management care, was not taken care of very well. It would be just horrible. If you walk on one of the wards ... If Pennhurst been still open, you would walk on the ward today and seen, you would say to yourself, "Is this how they treat these clients and these patients?" Unsanitry. Unfilthy. Beds unchangeable. People used to sleep not three or four covers, but they used to be bed wetting and sleep in their own filth. And low-grade clients used to be throwing soil at you. That was sickness. Some of the patients used to be tied to the benches — all day long in shackles, all day long in shackles, in restraints, all day long. Whoever want to be in restraints all day long and can't free themselves? It was awful sight to see. And this is how come that people didn't take a good look. I know a parent used to fuss at Pennhurst about Pennhurst about the horrible conditions that they have up there. That the conditions was very horrible. It was not like any other institution. I can't 'xplain any other way, but it was horrible, a horrible place. Like an animal in a zoo, locked up twenty-four hours; that's an awful thing to do; you can't do that with clients, with patients.

[S.B. asks how he got out of Pennhurst.]

I think that the important thing is to know that when you work around with people with disabilities that they sometimes they hard to get to know you — you got to know them very well. It's very hard for a person, if you bring them in your office, or talk to them, if you find out that somebody is very upset due cause they just came out of an institution, had been placed in the community. Sometimes they don't get to know you very well; and sometimes they do get frightened. Fears sometimes — I must instill this in you — because when I first came back out in the community I was scared for a little while. And after that it moved off and I wasn't scared no more. There are people that do get very very scared; sometimes they don't like to get near you sometimes …

APPENDIX: ROLAND'S LIFE

ROLAND JOHNSON
(1945-1994)

Pennhurst State School 1958-1971
Participant, CCH Partial Hospitalization Day Program 1978
President Philadelphia Chapter Speaking For Ourselve 1985
President Board of Directors Speaking
For Ourselves 1986-1990
Trainer in Self-Advocacy, Connecticut 1986
Speech: "Why Self-Advocates" at People First of Canada National
Retreat, Toronto 1986
Speech: "Real Jobs In The Community" at Speaking For Ourselves
4th Annual Conference, Philadelphia 1986
Speech: "The Role of Advocacy" at American Association of
Mental Retardation, Denver (first formal presentation by a person
with disabilities to the oldest professional organization concerned
with this disability) 1986
Speech at New York State Service Providers
Conference, Albany 1986
Guest Lecturer, Graduate School of Social Work at University of
Pennsylvania and at Temple University 1986-1991
Keynote Speaker at Pennhurst Closing Ceremony 1987

Guest on WHYY-FM in connection with the
closing of Pennhurst 1987
"A Just Reward For Perseverance" — subject of article by Steve
Lopez for *Philadelphia Inquirer* 1987
Trainer for National Park Service, Philadelphia 1988
Co-Facilitator: Second Annual Leadership Retreat,
Fellowship Farm 1988
Consultant for Work Interview Project at Temple University
(hired to survey peers regarding satisfaction with jobs in sheltered
workshops) 1988
Interview: "In Touch" (speaks with PA Secretary of Public Welfare
about community living on a videotape which was used in training
for 42,000 state employees) 1988
Testimony given in Federal Court, Philadelphia regarding
impact of funding crisis on plaintiffs in the on-going Pennhurst
case 1989
Award: Consumer Participation in Five State Region, American
Association of Mental Retardation 1989
Key Player in activity leading to Federal Court case which resulted
in people leaving Pinehill 1989
Co-Sponsor Voter Training with League of Women Voters,
Philadelphia 1989
Speech: National Accreditation Council on Developmental
Disabilities, Virginia 1989
Award: "Advocate of the Year," Montgomery County Association
for Retarded Citizens 1989
Co-Facilitator of Retreat sponsored by PA Office of Mental
Retardation, Hershey 1990
Special Guest: White House Ceremony at Signing of American With
Disabilities Act 1990
Speech: Self-Advocacy Session of American Association of Mental
Retardation Conference, Atlanta 1990

Key Participant in Peer Interview Project, published as "Hiring Consumers to Interview Consumers About Day Program Satisfaction and Hopes: A Pilot Test" by University of Haifa OMNAH Association for Developmentally Disabled People 1990
Speech: "The Role of Self-Advocacy" at First National People First Conference, Denver 1990
Elected North East Representative to National Steering Committee on Self-Advocacy, Denver 1991
Keynote Speaker: President's Committee on Mental Retardation, 25th Anniversary, Washington 1991
Speech: "Report on National Steering Committee" at Second National People First Conference, Nashville 1991
Leader: PA State-Wide Self-Advocacy Leadership Retreat, Fellowship Farm .... 1991 & 1992
Speaks on HIV/AIDS and People With Disabilities as Consultant for Philadelphia Coordinated Health Care to both disability and AIDS groups 1992-1993
Trainer at PA State-wide Self-Advocacy Leadership Retreat, ellowship Farm 1992
Member, PA council on Developmental Disabilities 1992-1993
Trainer on Self-Advocacy in PA, State College, Altoona, Pittsburgh, Harrisburg .... .1992
Speech: "Sounding the Warning: HIV Disease and Persons With Disabilities" at American Association on Mental Retardation Conference, New Orleans 1992
Interviewed for CNN's "Special Assignment" 1993
Presents Award to President Bush in connection with the A.D.A. (broadcast on "Nightline") 1993
Speech: "HIV/AIDS: Practical Approaches to Prevention and Service Delivery" at "Everyday Lives" State-wide Conference sponsored by the Commonwealth of Pennsylvania 1993
Speech: "Who's In Control?" at Third International People First Conference, Toronto 1993

THE PASSION OF ROLAND JOHNSON
by Robert Perske

A great man named Robert Penn Warren believed:

That if you really want to know a man,
You must know his passion.
I knew Roland Johnson because
I knew his passion.
He had lots of it.

Roland always spoke
With passion —
With that lovely wooing note in his voice,
That verbal beckoning finger
That drew you close
And made you listen to his hunger
For the dignity and freedom
For all of his friends.

Words failed him sometimes,
And his sentences got mixed up,
But not his urgency.
And I always got the point
Because I felt, really *felt* his passion.

Then I got to thinking how we rub elbows
With people who can have lots of smarts:

reading and writing smarts
adding and subtracting smarts
thinking and professional smarts ...

But they possess no passion.

* * *

So if the Good Lord came to me
And suddenly gave me the choice
Between having either
The smarts of the smarties
Or the passion of Roland Johnson ...

I would choose ... Roland's passion every time.

• • •

Bob Perske · 159 Hollow Tree Ridge Road · Darien, CT 06820

REMEMBERING ROLAND
by Susan Bartholomew and Carrol Reckard

The AIDS Memorial Quilt began with friends and family from the San Francisco area searching to find a way to communicate and help others understand the loss they were experiencing. In 1987 a group of people from that area got together and decided "to take all of their individual experiences, and stitch them together to make something that had strength and beauty." That is how the quilt started. It was a great success. Family and friends started to send quilt panels to San Francisco from all over the country. There are now over 29,000 panels.

The panels are three-foot by six-foot. Displays of portions of the quilt are held at various locations around the country. The entire quilt has been displayed on two occasions in Washington, D.C.

In the spring of 1994, Roland, Mary, Bill, Bobby, and Carrol with very mixed feelings went to see a part of the AIDS Memorial Quilt on exhibit at Ursinus College. Roland was quiet as he walked through the exhibit as they all tried to deal with the overwhelming meaning of what they saw there. Roland signed his name on the panel arranged on the floor that would be used to remember the exhibit at Ursinus and his four friends encircled his name with their own signatures. Roland was very taken by the fact that people made these quilts for someone who died from the HIV virus, and that people loved and cared for people who died of AIDS/HIV.

That night was the beginning of Roland's quilt. Roland suffered with HIV related illness for over eight years. During those years, Roland battled with nightmares but also worked on fulfilling his dreams. Those dreams included having his own home with a garden, where he could have friends over; staying in hotels with big beds and swimming pools; vacationing at Disney World as often as possible; becoming an important leader and speaker; having his friends and family around him; and having a committed partner. With a limited time, he risked challenging his fears. Roland's life changed with his HIV diagnosis — it became richer.

Little did his friends know on that 1994 Spring day that they would be making a quilt so soon. Roland's quilt is about his life. We used his favorite colors, and the things that mattered to him.

Family and friends were invited to contribute to the making of the quilt panel in memory of Roland. There were three themes: his church and family, his home and personal life, and Speaking for Ourselves and his public life. As part of the church and family theme, there were Bible verse needlepoints and the dove representing his Church. The appliqué of his house is surrounded by the things that mattered in his personal life, like his cat, Mittens, and the frog that hung on the bulletin board in his hospital room. The logo for Speaking for Ourselves, a self-advocacy organization, was used as the center of his public life; the gavel stood for the years he was president of the Philadelphia chapter of Speaking For Ourselves and for the four years that he was president of the Board, and vice president of the national self-advocacy organization.

Roland's friends and family dedicated the quilt in May of 1995 at the Armory. It was displayed there for the weekend along with 800 other quilt panels and 28 new panels from this area. Roland's panel was sent to San Francisco and is now part of the larger quilt.

The quilt can be viewed online at www.libertynet.org/speaking.

COMMISSIONER'S AWARD
Washington, D.C.

I first met Roland Johnson in the mid-1980's at the Regional Self-Advocacy Conference in New Jersey. By then, Roland had been out of Pennhurst for several years. But like Harriet Tubman, Roland kept going back, kept going back to places like Pennhurst to inspire people; to teach people about both their human and civil rights. And together with other leaders like Steve Dorsey and Pam Bard, Roland helped found and lead a group known aptly as "Speaking For Ourselves." Speaking For Ourselves is, indeed, a passionate voice for freedom in our country.

Roland was a brother. We lost him last year. With him we lost a hugely passionate and determined Black man who knew what justice is truly all about. We lost Roland, but he left a legacy and a charge which we must ponder by making our own today. Many of us looked to him and will continue to look to him as a leader who always sought out simple justice in everything he said and did. His death is not only a personal loss to those of us who knew him, nor a loss simply to the self-advocacy movement. It is a loss to all people seeking that same simple justice.

On September 15, 1995, Bob Williams, Commissioner on Developmental Disabilities, presented the Commissioner's Award in honor of Roland Johnson.

ROLAND

Standing on a vast box of a stage
your strong brown face framed
by a backdrop of glowing colours
of flags of many nations,
reflecting the rainbow of 1,000 faces
listening intently
as you urged

Take the power.
You must take the power.
The question is,
Who's in control?
Are we in control?
We have to take control.

I was already standing, mesmerized, tingling,
as people applauded,
clapping, smiling, singing, cheering,
raised hands in the air,
quietly nodded approval,
while a young woman insisted
that her attendant
wheel her chair closer to the stage.

You sat down,
Your face seemed to say,
"Did everybody really understand?"

I never did ask you since then
how you felt about that speech.
I would love to tell you

how I will always remember that moment,
as I will remember
how Martin Luther King
had a glorious dream.

We first met
one balmy summer day in Puget Sound
sitting on the soft green grass,
two conference participants,
I
the eager organizer
awe-struck by this new social movement,
You
the new leader.
You didn't say much then.

My memory of you then is faint.
That conference flattened me,
my mind overwhelmed by the mental emotional deluge
pounding against the walls
of my predetermined global analysis.

When you first came to Canada,
to see how we do our work up here,
you told us your story
in a daring
courageous
act of trust
how you spent most of your life
in a place called Pennhurst School.
We all knew there was a lot behind your careful words
when you said that it was not a very good place to live.
You were optimistic about the future.

Your optimism has always been wise
not frivolous.
I have learned from your wisdom,
unlearned a few things too.
I especially learned to question myself.

Years later
we talked
in a Philadelphia restaurant;
a memory seared in my heart.
You insisted on buying me lunch.
After egg rolls you told me
your voice calm and gentle
how you were HIV positive
and everything was okay
that I shouldn't worry.

You were so kind to me.
I never did have a chance
to thank you for that.
I cried
because I was losing you
because I was moved by your strength.

Your mission continued
as respected national leader
known by powerful people;
a personal example of dignity
and determination;
an advocate
who must be consulted on policies
for people with disabilities.
And now

speaking out about AIDS.

Some say you pushed yourself too much
But I guess there were those who thought
Martin was crazy to go to Memphis
that Malcolm should have just laid low for awhile.
Who are we to say what is safe
what is right
to those who are driven by majestic dreams
even as the darkness of death
appears on the horizon.

I heard stories from loyal friends
about your last days
in a hospital room.
You made sure you had control
over that benevolent dictatorship
of white coats and computerized contraptions,
and other people's desires,
until you quietly
ceded control
where every human being
has no power.

I will miss you Roland.
Your spirit and your dreams
fill my being with glowing power.
Can I ever be as strong as you?

—*Bill Worrell*

A SPECIAL FRIEND

My personal relationship with Roland Johnson was a superb one. As a person with a disability, Roland was a great inspiration to me. He understood what people with disabilities were trying to do for themselves. He gave me hope in whatever I decided to do for the group of SELF-ADVOCATES BECOMING EMPOWERED and People First of Ruston. He lived a good life for all people with disabilities to look up to now and forever!

Roland spoke very strongly about standing up for yourself and demanding due respect as a person and not allowing "normal" people to dominate us. I believe that he would have liked to see the institutions closed today and put people in group homes where they can learn more about independence and what it is like to have a Family and JOBS now!

I wish he could have seen that we are closing institutions today!

—*Kammie Barfield, Secretary*
Self-Advocates Becoming Empowered
May 23, 1996

IN HIS MEMORY: A GREAT LEADER

Dignity
Solidity
Nobility
Humility
Honesty
Clarity
Credibility

Ability to pinpoint
Culpability with diplomacy

not accepting futility
of labeled disability
Promoter of another's
Leadership Ability

unrelenting Tenacity
rigorously imposed
Self-Accountability

We all wanted to believe
In Roland's invincibility
Putting off
Inevitability

Vulnerability
Fragility
Reality and
Undeniability
of Mortality

Mortality but not Finality
of Powerful Spirituality

—*Bill Worrell*

ROLAND JOHNSON
Reprinted from The Community Services Reporter

Editor's Note: Roland Johnson died two months ago. From 1986 to 1990, he was President of Speaking For Ourselves, a Philadelphia-based self-advocacy organization. In 1992, he served as Vice President of Self-Advocates Becoming Empowered, a national self-advocacy organization. He advised the Pennsylvania Office of Mental Retardation and appeared on local and national television programs. Roland Johnson was a powerful advocate for people with disabilities. He taught countless people about disability and helped his colleagues "speak out so they could be in charge."

Nancy Thaler, Pennsylvania's Deputy Secretary for Mental Retardation, shares her thoughts about Roland Johnson in an open letter:

Dear Friends and Colleagues:

Even as I write this greeting, I can hear Roland Johnson say the word "colleague" with his powerful voice. It is with sadness that I write this open letter.

Many times in our lives we are so absorbed in our own activity of living that we fail to learn about some significant event, or if we do, do not comprehend its significance. This must not happen in our community in the case of Roland Johnson.

Roland Johnson, a nationally recognized advocate for people with disabilities, died on August 29th, 1994 of cardiac arrest. He was 48 years old and lived in Collegeville, Pennsylvania.

Roland was a hero and a leader, and it is important for those who did not have the pleasure of knowing him, working with him or hearing him speak, to know about him and what he has left us.

Roland lived with his family until age of 12, and was then admitted to Pennhurst Center. He experienced the frustration of losing his family, because they did not have the knowledge and support to raise him, and the horror of institutional living. Roland's spirit was powerful and he turned these experiences into compassion for families with children with disabilities and a passion to get everyone out of institutions and give people control over their lives.

Roland challenged his colleagues to take control over their lives. He was often heard in speeches to shout, "Who's in control? Are you in control or is the staff in control?" The challenge was also directed at the help givers; a wake-up call.

Roland was a pioneer. It is impossible to know the courage of a man who had slung at him the worst labels and insults imaginable, who suffered abuse and neglect, and who belonged to a group totally discounted by society, but who nevertheless stood up in public to speak for himself and his people.

Roland gave voice to the people. Roland made us listen. Roland changed how we think about disabilities. Roland showed us what forgiveness and generosity are, and Roland showed us what courage and dignity look like.

Other heroes like Frederick Douglass, Harriet Tubman, and Susan B. Anthony passed from life to be forgotten for a time because they came from a group that was devalued by mainstream society, only to be discovered and valued by later generations. This does not have to happen to Roland Johnson.

If we care about all people and the struggle for social justice, we have to hold on to our heroes and so hold Roland in our hearts ... and create opportunities and support for others to speak, and then listen to them.

Sincerely,

Nancy R. Thaler

WE'LL BE THINKING OF YOU

I remember how you helped me see
That I was someone
That there was something good in me
You changed my life
Just look at all the things I do
I'll remember I'll remember you

CHORUS: We'll be thinking we'll be thinking of you
We'll be thinking we'll be thinking of you
Always
We'll be thinking we'll be thinking of you

The way you spoke out when you saw something wrong
The way you stood fast
Though the struggle lasts so long
It was your voice
Put us on the right track
Now you've gone away but we're never turning back

CHORUS

When we speak out when we stand up for our rights
When we find the strength we need
To go on with the fight
When we stand together
And help each other through
We'll be thinking we'll be thinking of you

CHORUS

© *Karl Williams [This song has been recorded by Speaking For Ourselves. It is also included on the CD "Respect: Songs of the Self-Advocacy Movement" by Self-Advocates Becoming Empowered (SABE)]*

About the Authors

After spending half his childhood in Pennhurst State School and Hospital for the Mentally Retarded, **Roland Johnson** emerged to become a captivating speaker and a respected leader of the self-advocacy movement. The story of the path he traveled and of the people who helped him along the way is a testament to the triumph of the human spirit and the power of good will as a strategy for effecting social change.

Speaking For Ourselves is a Philadelphia-based organization with chapters across Pennsylvania. Run by people with developmental disabilities, its mission is to speak out on important issues, to provide support for its members, and to teach the public about the needs, wishes, and potential of people with disabilities.

Karl Williams is a musician and a writer.